GREAT WAR LITERATURE

STUDY GUIDE

Written by W Lawrance

on

WAR POETS

OF THE FIRST WORLD WAR

VOLUME ONE

Great War Literature Study Guide on War Poets of the First World War - Volume One
Written by W Lawrance

Published by:
Great War Literature Publishing LLP
Darrington Lodge, Springfield Road, Camberley, Surrey GU15 1AB Great Britain
Web site: *www.greatwarliterature.co.uk*
E-Mail: *editor@greatwarliterature.co.uk*

First Published December 2005
Reprinted 2006, 2007, 2008

Produced in Great Britain

ISBN 9781905378241 (1905378246) Paperback Edition

Design and production by Great War Literature Publishing LLP
Typeset in Gill Sans and Trajan Pro

War Poets of the First World War - Volume One

CONTENTS

PREFACE

Great War Literature Study Guides' primary purpose is to provide in-depth analysis of First World War literature for GCSE and A-Level students.

There are plenty of other study guides available and while these make every effort to help with the analysis of war literature, they do so from a more general overview perspective.

Great War Literature Publishing have taken the positive decision to produce a more detailed and in-depth interpretation of selected works for students. We also actively promote the publication of our works in an electronic format via the Internet to give the broadest possible access.

Our publications can be used in isolation or in collaboration with other study guides. It is our aim to provide assistance with your understanding of First World War literature, not to provide the answers to specific questions. This approach provides the resources that allow the student the freedom to reach their own conclusions and express an independent viewpoint.

Great War Literature Study Guides can include elements such as biographical detail, historical significance, character assessment, synopsis of text, and analysis of poetry and themes.

The structure of Great War Literature Study Guides allows the reader to delve into a required section easily without the need to read from beginning to end. This is especially true of our e-Books.

The Great War Literature Study Guides have been thoroughly researched and are the result of over 20 years of experience of studying this particular genre.

Studying literature is not about being right or wrong, it is entirely a matter of opinion. The secret to success is developing the ability to form these opinions and to deliver them succinctly and reinforce them with quotes and clear references from the text.

Great War Literature Study Guides help to extend your knowledge of First World War literature and offer clear definitions and guidance to enhance your studying. Our clear and simple layouts make the guides easy to access and understand.

HOW TO STUDY POETRY

This might sound like quite a simple process, but in order to get the best out of reading and understanding poetry, here are a few tips:

1. Firstly, although this sounds obvious, read the poem through. You may not understand it the first time you read it, or you may think it is crystal clear - either way, it doesn't matter. Think about what you have read.

2. Then re-read the poem, but this time much more slowly, and, if possible, out load. Pay particular attention to any passages which you don't understand. Now make some notes on the parts which you do understand, and possible explanations, if you have any, for the more complicated passages.

3. Once you have written your notes, re-read the poem again. See if your perspective changes or whether you can understand the poem more clearly. At this point, I would suggest you start using the Study Guide to either re-inforce your opinions or help analyse the sections of poetry with which you are struggling.

4. We, deliberately, have not stressed too much importance on the literary form of the poems as this not a matter of opinion or conjecture. The form of a poem is able to be deduced from an understanding of literary terminology. Therefore, for your information, there is a Literary Glossary of terms available on our Web site at: www.greatwarliterature.co.uk/glossary.html

5. Some poets' work is easier to understand than others and, for this reason, it is essential that you have a thorough understanding of the poets themselves, which is why, in the Great War Literature Study Guides, the biographical detail always comes first.

INTRODUCTION

The poetry of the First World War can be read as simply that: poetry. However, and much more interestingly, it can be viewed as a commentary of one of the most catastrophic events in history. The First World War ended many lives and those who survived found that most of what they believed they were fighting for had vanished in the mud of Flanders. The poetry of that era charts these changing times: from Rupert Brooke's patriotic *1914* sonnets, to Siegfried Sassoon's final plea that the dead of the war should never been forgotten. In between there was a wealth of poetry which demonstrates how and why the attitude of so many changed from youthful enthusiasm to hopeless disillusionment.

It is essential for any student of First World War poetry to see the poems they are studying through the eyes of those who wrote them. To assist with this, Great War Literature Poetry Study Guides contain detailed biographies of each of the poets concerned. Their opinions and experiences shaped the way they wrote and many poems are based on real-life events, the knowledge and understanding of which can only enhance one's appreciation of their work.

Knowing, for example, that Wilfred Owen really did spend a freezing cold winter in the trenches, makes his writing of *Exposure* seem even more realistic and understandable. Equally, realising that Siegfried Sassoon witnessed a scene just like the one he describes in *Lamentations* helps to make sense of this poem and gives it a more human touch. Just as interesting, however, is the knowledge that the poet who wrote some of the most realistic trench-life poems, Wilfrid Wilson Gibson, never left Britain's shores during the conflict.

Armed with the knowledge gained through these biographies, many students will be able to begin analysing the poetry for themselves and to assist with this, we have provided in-depth analysis for each poet's major works. These are not designed to give a definitive answer, simply because there isn't one. Our guides are intended to give students a place from which to start, or a means of reinforcing already-formed opinions and, hopefully, create a new generation whose appreciation of this poetry is equal to that which it, and its creators, deserve.

RUPERT BROOKE

BIOGRAPHY

Rupert Chawner Brooke began his tragically short life on 3rd August 1887. His father, William, was a classics master at Rugby, where Rupert and his two brothers Richard and William were all born. His domineering mother, Mary, ensured that Rupert and his two brothers enjoyed a comfortable and secure childhood.

Rupert entered Rugby School as a boarder in 1901, becoming a popular and well-rounded student. His success in the classroom was matched by manly heroics on the sports field - he played cricket and rugby, as well as winning the school poetry prize in 1905. He was an extremely handsome young man - tall, with classical good-looks and a mane of red-gold hair.

In 1906, Brooke left Rugby, bound for King's College, Cambridge, having won a classical scholarship. He lived an idyllic 'Georgian' life of outings, picnics and boating on the Cam - essentially typifying the essence of the upper classes in the 'golden' age of pre-war England. He also embarked on a series of unsuccessful love affairs. Rupert was a young man who fell passionately in love and upon the failure of these relationships, became suicidally depressed. On one such occasion, he wrote to a girlfriend (Noel Olivier) that if she continued to refuse to marry him, he would kill himself, such was his desperation. Noel, a sensible young lady, ignored this emotional blackmail and adamantly stated that she would never marry him.

During his final year at University, he moved to the Old Vicarage in Grantchester, making a determined effort to succeed with his degree.

1910 found Rupert back at Rugby, where, following the death of his father, he stood in for a term as temporary housemaster. He then began working on a thesis on Webster and the Elizabethan dramatists. At around this time, he embarked on yet another unsuccessful love affair with Katharine Cox, the failure of which shattered his happy existence and saw him leave England for France and Germany. In May 1912, while travelling, he wrote his most famous pre-war poem, *The Old Vicarage, Grantchester*, which he originally entitled *The Sentimental Exile*. This poem evokes the archetypal Edwardian England which, had he but known it, was soon to be lost forever.

Returning to England in December 1912, Brooke entered into a whirl of social engagements. His circle of friends, by this time, included Edward Marsh (secretary to Winston Churchill and prominent literary figure), Arthur and Violet Asquith (children of the Prime Minister), E. M. Forster, Virginia Woolf and actress Catherine Nesbitt with whom he had fallen in love.

Edward Marsh was a friend to many poets, including Siegfried Sassoon and Wilfrid Wilson Gibson, and he, Gibson and Brooke collaborated on the *Georgian Anthology* of poems. Gibson and Brooke went on to become close friends, with Brooke referring to Gibson as "Wibson".

In March 1913, Brooke learned that, as a result of his dissertation on Webster, he had been awarded a fellowship at Kings. Later that spring he sailed for America and Canada and then proceeded to New Zealand, where he spent Christmas. Early in 1914 he travelled to Tahiti, where he met and fell in love with a beautiful Samoan girl called Taatamata.

In June 1914 Brooke returned, once again, to England and during the following month, Edward Marsh introduced him to Siegfried Sassoon, who was, by now living in London in rooms very near to Marsh. Also in July Marsh and Brooke dined with the Prime Minister, Herbert Asquith and Brooke was introduced to Winston Churchill, then First Lord of the Admiralty. With the prospect of war looming, Churchill offered to assist Brooke with obtaining a commission. The young poet was, however, unsure in which direction the forthcoming conflict should take him - initially contemplating travelling to France to help bring in the harvests.

Following the declaration of war on the 4th August 1914, Brooke decided that he should be involved and, with Marsh's assistance, gained a commission in the Royal Naval Division as a Sub-Lieutenant. On 4th October he set sail, with his battalion, Anson, bound for Antwerp to halt the German advance through Belgium. This exercise proved a failure - Antwerp was lost and Brooke and his battalion joined the Belgian refugees fleeing the advancing Germans. By 9th October he was back in England. This was to prove Brooke's only military experience of the First World War, but it had a profound and lasting effect. He was deeply troubled by the sights he had witnessed, particularly the suffering of the Belgian people and this made him determined to right the wrongs he felt had been done to them.

Brooke transferred from Anson to Hood battalion. At the end of November, the battalion, including Brooke and Arthur Asquith, with whom he served, was moved to Blandford Camp in Dorset. It was around this time that he began working on his five sonnets which would make him famous. When these were completed, early in 1915, he sent them to Wilfrid Gibson.

A bout of illness in early February saw Brooke become a resident patient at No. 10 Downing Street, where he was nursed back to health by Violet Asquith. By the 28th of that month, however, Brooke had taken leave of his friends and was aboard the *Grantully Castle*, bound for Gallipoli. This was an interesting journey which included dining at the Union Club in Malta and enjoying a performance of Tosca, as well as an expedition to see the Pyramids and the Sphinx.

The beginning of April was the beginning of the end for Brooke. He became sick and spent several days confined to his bed on a strict diet of arrowroot. He also developed a sore on his upper lip. Gradually, however, his health seemed to improve, the sore disappeared and he returned to duty. The *Grantully Castle* had, by now, returned to Lemnos and, while anchored in the Bay of Skyros, Brooke received a letter from Edward Marsh informing him that his sonnet, *The Soldier*, had been read out during a sermon in St Pauls Cathedral and had subsequently appeared in *The Times*.

On the evening of 20th April, Brooke complained of feeling unwell - the sore on his lip had returned - and he retired early to bed. By the following day, his health had deteriorated rapidly - he ached all over, drifted in and out of consciousness and had an extremely high temperature. Several surgeons and medical officers examined him and agreed that the cause of his problem was an infected mosquito bite. Despite his removal to a French hospital ship and the surgeon's attempts to save him, Rupert Brooke died on the afternoon of St George's Day, 23rd April 1915.

In a hastily arranged funeral, Brooke was buried in an olive grove on the island of Skyros, surrounded by his friends. The blow to Rupert's family was compounded by the death, less than nine weeks later, of his younger brother William, who was serving on the Western front as a Second Lieutenant with the London Regiment (Post Office Rifles).

Rupert's untimely death gave the nation a focus, fuelled by his friends who quickly sought to bring his work to the attention of the public at large. During and immediately after the war, his poems sold in vast numbers.

More recently, many have decried his work as sentimental and unrealistic but it should be remembered that at this time, Wilfred Owen's was writing equally fervent and patriotic verse, as indeed were Siegfried Sassoon and many of the other poets who would later become better known for their bitter or angry poetry.

Even in death, the loyal Brooke remembered his friends. He had always been aware that Wilfrid Wilson Gibson lived in dire financial straits and made him, along with Walter de la Mare and Lascelles Abercrombie, a legatee of his literary estate. The royalties received from the sale of Brooke's poems ensured that Gibson's financial problems were over.

With such a limited experience of war, Rupert Brooke is probably better described as a 'pre-war' poet, than a war poet; his sonnets are realistic representations of his era. Had he lived, he could well have gone on to write equally realistic trench-life poems. His sonnets perfectly encapsulate the qualities of his time and the pride and patriotism then displayed by so many young men.

POETRY ANALYSIS

INTRODUCTION

Brooke's collection of sonnets, entitled *1914*, are treated here individually under their own titles. The themes and language used by Brooke are, essentially, the same throughout the five sonnets. He uses gentle, peaceful language which demonstrates his sense that death will ultimately bring freedom and harmony and that dying for one's country is an honour.

There are no bullets or bayonets here, no rotting corpses, no stench. He had not experienced any of these things, and therefore, he chose not to write about them. His poems reflect his participation in the war up to that point and his patriotic beliefs, which, however we might look at them now, were commonly held at that time.

I. PEACE

This sonnet begins by drawing our attention to the fact that Brooke feels that the youth of England is perfectly suited to the challenge that lies ahead. He thanks God for allowing his generation the opportunity to serve their country in this fashion. His sense that England's youth has been slumbering shows that he may have felt his life had little purpose before the war. This was a commonly held concept amongst the upper class young men of the day whose pursuits could now be said to be "idle". The war, it would seem, gave them a purpose.

He goes on, in the next two lines, to demonstrate the keen athletic powers of these eminently suitable young men, who will turn away from the idle pursuits of their youth, and embrace a better, cleaner future. This shows his sense that the assured victory (which most people saw as a foregone conclusion) will ensure the future of his nation. He seems to imply that the country will be made clean or strong, by this victory, suggesting that he perceives that pre-war England lacked these qualities, and that it is the duty of his generation to return the nation to a former glory.

This is re-iterated by his suggestion that these men will be glad to leave behind the old world which has become tired and careless. They will also happily turn their backs on those who have not had the honour to enlist and serve their country. The final line of this stanza, which refers to love as being empty could be a reflection of his failed pre-war love affairs, which in the grand scheme of things he now perceives as insignificant, although at the time their failure had made him extremely depressed. This shows how his priorities have now changed.

The second stanza refers to the magnitude of war and death: nothing is important, or for that matter even exists - not illness or grief - only death. However, death is described more in terms of a long peaceful sleep, rather than the end of life. This is a not the violent, horrifying death of Wilfred Owen's *Dulce Et Decorum Est;* this instead is the picture of a glorious death: bringing release. He believes that in death the heart will find happiness, which demonstrates that, to him, life had, perhaps, become a source of unhappiness. He admits that there may be pain to be endured before the final freedom of death, but even that will eventually end. The pain to which he refers, however, might be a reference to the grief which those who are left behind may feel. In this case, he seems to understand that this sense of loss will not last forever and will eventually be relieved.

This poem, like many of Brooke's, shows the poet's idea that the war has given England's youth the opportunity to sacrifice itself for the greater good of their country, and that such a sacrifice is the only noble and just course of action for a young man to take. Such nationalist pride was quite common in the early days, and even years, of the First World War. Brooke does not speak of bullets or bayonets, in fact his image of death is quite serene - like a man simply falling asleep.

He sees death as an enemy, but also as a friend, implying that to sacrifice himself in this way, although it would remove him from his loved-ones, would also grant him the ultimate fulfilment of his life. This also suggests that, to him, death - as a friend - provides a means of escape, either from his own existence, or from a world in which he possibly feels that, without the honour of either a noble death, or a victory, he would have no future.

II. SAFETY

This poem, simply, demonstrates the feeling of security that Brooke felt, once he had decided that his death was almost inevitable. Winston Churchill said at the time that he sensed that Brooke had expected and was, indeed, willing to die for his beloved and beautiful England.

This sonnet tells of Brooke's sense that he has found safety and security in the knowledge that his death will perpetuate life. In other words, through his death, a way of life can be allowed to carry on. Natural events, such as dawn, birdsong, and clouds scudding across the sky will all continue despite the enriching experience of his death.

The achievements of his generation, he states, will not diminish with the passage of time. Death, or the fear of death, cannot harm him - it will instead be an enriching experience and one which will bring him ultimate security and safety, and even happiness, in a world now free of pain. When pitched against this sense of satisfaction, he believes that war is powerless - it cannot harm you if you are not afraid of its consequences.

The fact that he no longer fears his own death has provided him with a secret inner security. Instead, he believes that death will afford him the ultimate safety - the knowledge that through the giving of his life, he has provided a future for his country.

This sentiment is reminiscent of Julian Grenfell's *Into Battle*, in which he states that those who die in war will be made greater by their experience and their sacrifices. Grenfell's poem ends with the dead being folded in the soft wings of the night, which echoes the sense of security in death portrayed here by Rupert Brooke.

III. THE DEAD

Like Brooke's other *1914* Sonnets, this poem again emphasises the honour of dying for one's country. Even those who were poor (not in a monetary sense, but in the sense of having a worthless or empty life), have been enriched by death - given gifts more rare and valuable, than gold. The gifts they have been given are the knowledge that their sacrifice has not been in vain and that they have served their country. He uses the word "us", emphasising that he felt his own pre-war existence had little purpose.

Unlike in his other poems, though, Brooke points out that these sacrifices, although worthwhile, are not without cost. These men, he says have given up their youth and their future - a career, old age and the opportunity to have children - or to have "a life". He implies, however, that what they have done - the sacrifice they have made - has earned them a place in history - their immortality.

In the second stanza, he reiterates this by saying that these deaths have enabled the earth to effectively, be reborn. Honour, Holiness and Nobleness exist again in the world. These have been earned by the sacrifice of a generation - but he insists that this is what they were born for - this was their heritage. It is almost as though he were saying that they were put on earth, at this moment in history, specifically to right the wrongs of previous generations and return the earth to its former glory. The war has given young men, he states, the opportunity to prove themselves worthy.

Again, this sentiment was fairly common at the beginning of the First World War. Many young men believed that it was their duty to protect their loved ones, their king and their country from the enemy. Brooke's language in his poems turned this sense of national pride into a serene crusade to bring goodness back to the earth again.

IV. THE DEAD

The first stanza of this sonnet reflects the simple joy of a youthful generation. The small, often insignificant, experiences of their short lives are listed as though they are wondrous. Everything from the witnessing of sunset and dawn, to sleeping and waking, or the simplicity of touching a flower in bloom, are used to demonstrate the sacrifice that this generation has made, now that their lives are over. They have willingly given up all of these pleasures. None of this is said with an element of regret or bitterness, however - even the sorrows of these men are seen as marvellous - everything is an experience, even sadness. Instead Brooke uses these examples to show the shining nature of youth.

The second verse reiterates how death has changed everything. The waters represent the men, who in life had discovered laughter and richness through their noble deeds, but now, in death, they lie still, as though frozen. Even then, though, Brooke paints death as an image of beauty - despite his references to frost, which is often used by poets to demonstrate the bitter cold and pointlessness of death, here it is seen as shining and peaceful - like a frozen lake - radiant under the moonlight. Again, Brooke's dead are glorious and, though their sacrifices have found peace.

The language which Brooke uses gives the impression of an island, surrounded by water, which could either be a reference to man or to Britain as an island. The mens' hearts are washed, and in death he likens them to water - they were waves that danced and have been stopped only by the frost of death. In their wake, however, they leave a glorious, shining peace for the world to enjoy.

V. THE SOLDIER

This is Brooke's most famous and frequently quoted poem. It is unashamedly patriotic - he mentions the words 'England' or 'English' six times in just fourteen lines of verse. Simply put, this sonnet demonstrates that Brooke feels that, whatever happens to him - wherever he ends up - he will always be proud to have been born an Englishman.

Again, as in his other sonnets, he paints a picture of English serenity. He believes that it is his nationality which has made him the person that he is and his strong patriotic feelings shine through, above all else in this poem.

Even death, he believes, cannot remove that sense of pride from him and his passing will not be in vain if, at home in England people are, once again happy and at peace. He feels that by his death he will have given back to England everything, and more, that it gave to him. The happiness and security earned by his sacrifice will buy his eternal peace.

This beautiful poem evokes the idealistic image of a perfect England in a 'golden' age, such as many believe existed immediately prior to the First World War.

This poem has also come in for some criticism, over the years. Many feel that in *The Soldier*, Brooke places too much importance on his own sacrifices. Among those who believed this were Edward Thomas and Charles Hamilton Sorley, who, in their poems, placed more importance on the general sacrifices being made by so many, and on the loss of a way of life which the war would bring about.

Such criticisms may carry some merit, but should not detract from the fact that Brooke's *1914* Sonnets struck a chord at the time, with many who felt that to fight and die for one's country was justifiable. It became one of the most popular poems of the war, selling over 300,000 copies during the ensuing ten years. Its popularity only waned when the more realistic war memoirs began to be published.

WILFRID WILSON GIBSON

BIOGRAPHY

Wilfrid Wilson Gibson was born on 2nd October 1878 at Hexham in Northumberland. His father was a pharmacist, who, in his spare time, was also a writer and historian. Wilfrid attended local schools, but his father and sister were mainly responsible for his education. His upbringing, whilst happy and middle-class, was by no means privileged. Despite having, by many of his contemporaries' standards a less than remarkable education, Wilfrid's ambitions to write were so powerful that no career other than that of professional poet was even considered.

His early attempts at poetry were unsuccessful, being not very realistic studies of ancient legends. He decided to try writing from observation and soon found a cause which formed an excellent subject for his work, namely, the plight of the poor, working classes. He wrote in plain language, appealing to the increasing numbers of socially conscious, literate people. These poems are realistic, and the style which he developed at this time would later form the basis for his war poetry. He proved, however, that a poet does not necessarily have to experience his subject in order to write about it convincingly.

Many of these early works were published in *The Spectator* and Wilfrid went on to write plays, such as, *Stonefolds, Daily Bread* and *Fires* between 1907 and 1912. Other poems were printed in the literary magazine *Rhythm*, which was edited by Katherine Mansfield and John Middleton Murry. In the summer of 1912, Wilfrid decided to move to London where Mansfield and Middleton Murry found him accommodation and introduced him to other literary figures of the time, such as Ezra Pound and the influential Edward Marsh.

In September 1912, Marsh, who had taken an instant liking to Wilfrid, introduced him to Rupert Brooke. A friendship was immediately formed and Brooke soon came to refer to Gibson, with affection, as "Wibson".

Later that same month came the idea, formed ostensibly by Marsh and Brooke, of an anthology of poetry which became known as *Georgians*. Gibson was included amongst the poets in the first of these anthologies and his circle of literary friends soon enlarged. In October, he stayed with Brooke at The Old Vicarage in Grantchester.

Despite his success and popularity, Wilfrid was struggling financially. Marsh secretly assisted by paying him £1.00 per week to edit *Rhythm*. In November, Gibson moved into a bedsit above Harold Monro's Poetry Bookshop in Bloomsbury. Monro was a poet himself, but had also turned to publishing and was responsible for the production of Marsh's *Georgian* anthologies. The bedsit in which Gibson now resided would later be home to, amongst others, Robert Frost and Wilfred Owen.

Gibson was now introduced by Marsh to many more of London's literary figures and his poetry received great accolades. His position at *Rhythm* ended when that magazine ceased publication, but he was, by now, receiving royalty cheques for both *Georgians* and *Daily Bread*. In October 1913, he and Lascelles Abercrombie (another of Marsh's *Georgian* poets) went to stay in Florence where they met D H Lawrence.

By now, however, Wilfrid had fallen in love. The object of his affection was Harold Monro's secretary, Geraldine Townsend, and the couple were married in Dublin, near the home of Geraldine's parents, in November 1913.

Wilfrid and Geraldine decided to move to the country and settled in Dymock in Gloucestershire. Here, as well as being visited by Marsh and Brooke, the Gibsons became friends with other literary 'locals' such as Robert Frost and Edward Thomas. There were frequent gatherings of the 'Dymock Group' at which new ideas were often hatched. Among these was a suggestion for a quarterly magazine entitled *New Numbers* of which Wilfrid became editor.

Upon the outbreak of the First World War, many of the group enlisted. Gibson was rejected, four times, by the recruiting authorities, due to his poor eyesight. He continued with his writing, however, and before long had produced, among others, his poem *Breakfast.*

In April 1915 came dreadful news: Rupert Brooke was dead. Gibson was deeply affected by the loss of his dear friend and wrote poems in his memory. These were published, with others, in Gibson's collection *Friends* in 1916. As well as his poetry, Brooke left another legacy: he made Gibson, Lascelles Abercrombie and Walter de la Mare legatees of his literary estate. Brooke had always known of the precarious state of his friends' finances and this generous gesture ensured that, for Gibson, monetary worries were a thing of the past. He was now able to write more freely, without continually worrying about his financial situation.

In 1917, Gibson embarked on a popular lecture tour in America, reading and discussing Brooke's poems. Upon his return, he attempted to enlist again, and this time was successful. He initially became a driver with the Army Service Corps, then transferred to a job as clerk to a medical officer.

Gibson never saw active service overseas and after his demobilisation in 1919, he returned to his private life. He and

Geraldine had two children, Michael and Audrey and he continued to write poetry until the 1950s. He died on 26th May 1962, aged eighty-three.

Like his pre-war work, Gibson's war poetry represents the ordinary soldier, and displays his talent for capturing the essence of the working man. His war poetry has caused much confusion: so realistic are his tone and language that many of his readers and critics were convinced (and some remain so), that he was a 'soldier-poet' writing with first-hand experience of the front line.

Thanks, at least in part, to Brooke's generosity, Gibson was able to leave a legacy of his own: poems which, despite his non-combatant status, realistically reflect the plight of ordinary First World War soldiers.

Many 'soldier-poets' did not start writing realistic poetry until the war affected them personally - for example, Sassoon's poetry changed after the deaths of his brother Hamo and his friend David Thomas. The thing that distinguishes Gibson's work is that the war did not intrude into his life in the same way - he did not have the personal experience of trench life, or witnessing, first-hand, the death of a comrade, or having to kill a fellow human-being; and yet the truth and realism which shine through his poetry are as clear as if he had been there.

POETRY ANALYSIS

BREAKFAST

The title of this poem indicates an element of the ordinary, which serves to lull the reader into thinking that what follows will be a description of the men eating breakfast and initially, that is what this poem is. The men, we are told, must eat lying down, since there are shells flying over their heads. They discuss football, and one of them places a bet as to which team will win, especially if one particular player is going to play in the match. Another man takes this bet, lifts his head and is killed. The remaining men return to their breakfast.

Like much of Gibson's work, *Breakfast* describes mundane everyday events in the life of the ordinary private soldier. His description of their position during their meal, indicates the discomfort which the soldiers must endure probably every minute of the day. He is implying that, as even their meals cannot be taken in a normal manner, what hope is there for comfort in any other aspect of their lives.

This theme continues as we learn that, while eating, the men discuss a football match. Such discussions remind us that the men are thinking of home and that, despite the harshness of their surroundings, they have not stopped behaving like normal young men. One can imagine, in peacetime, these men having a similar wager while in a pub, or after work. At home, however, their bet would probably have been made with money, or beer. At the front, although they may well have had money, they bet a rasher of bacon against a loaf of bread. This serves to remind us how the simple, everyday items, which at home would have been taken for granted, now have a more special significance.

The bet is accepted by a man named Ginger, which is obviously a nickname. The use of this, rather than the man's real name, demonstrates the close attachments formed by the men. As well as friendships created in the trenches, there were many Pals Battalions - men who lived or worked together at home and who joined up en-masse. For example, by September 1915, Hull (a town which Gibson mentions in *Breakfast*), had four such Battalions. The implication of using the man's nickname, is that these men may have known each other even before the war.

Sometimes poets do not give names to the characters in their work - for example, *A Private* by Edward Thomas, *The Deserter* by Gilbert Frankau or *Suicide in the Trenches* by Siegfried Sassoon. Such anonymity serves many purposes: it can demonstrate that the name of the person is not as important as the message in the poem; or it may be used ironically to demonstrate the quantity of nameless dead, or the seeming unimportance of the soldiers themselves. This can also be used as a means of making a poem intentionally impersonal.

In *Breakfast*, however, Gibson is trying to achieve the opposite effect. By using a nickname, he is reinforcing the message that these men cared deeply about one another. Another example of this is *Comrades: An Episode* by Robert Nichols, which describes an officers attempts to drag his wounded body back to his trench so that he can see his men before he dies.

Having given the reader the impression that, despite their obvious discomforts and hardships, the men remain cheerful, Gibson shocks us with the abruptness of Ginger's death. He does not sentimentalise this event, but states it simply as a matter of fact. This reinforces the impression that death is an everyday occurrence, just like eating breakfast or discussing football.

The other men make no move, or comment on his death, but return to their breakfast. This could be said to demonstrate the men's sense of denial. This sentiment can also be seen in, for example, Sassoon's *Suicide in the Trenches*. By giving Ginger's death an air of insignificance, Gibson is pointing out that, at the front, there are so many men dying, that it is impossible to mourn each one individually, regardless of one's personal feelings. This, together with the repetition of the first two lines of the poem, shows how, despite the death and destruction surrounding them, for the living, life continues as before. Such repetition also demonstrates the monotony of the soldiers' lives.

Surprisingly, Gibson wrote *Breakfast* quite early in the war. It was written at a time when many other poets were still writing in idealistic tones, urging others to join the fight. In a few lines, Gibson manages to create an image which is harsh and realistic. To achieve this so early in the war, and without any first-hand experience, makes this poem quite remarkable.

IN THE AMBULANCE

The poem begins with a rhyme which gives the reader a false sense of security. This feeling is then dashed in the second and third verses, when we learn that the man chanting the rhyme is seriously injured. The wounded man, without consideration for anyone else, is repeating this rhyme throughout the night. He has lost both his legs, and presumably, due to loss of blood, has become light-headed. Finally the poem ends with the continued repetition of the rhyme.

The scene in this poem is set in an ambulance, which we learn only from the title. Gibson's economic use of words makes no allowance for scene-setting within the poem, so he uses the title for that purpose. The chant which the wounded man mutters is reminiscent of a nursery rhyme, and this gives the poem a sense of familiarity, home and security.

The jaunty air of the poem is continued into the second and third verses, but now the language no longer fits with the light, almost humourous tone of the first stanza. This change to a use of harsh language, particularly in the third verse, whilst using a brisk rhyme is particularly well done in this poem and helps to reinforce the strangeness of the injured man's situation. Gibson's poem is especially effective in making the reader really think about the wounded soldier's position. He achieves this by making the reader believe they are reading a nursery rhyme, and then juxtaposing this with the fact that this man no longer has any legs.

There is no outward sympathy shown for the injured man, in fact the impression created is that he is a nuisance because his chanting keeps the other men in the ambulance awake. He is using this rhyme to try to take his mind off his terrible injuries, probably also as a means of remaining conscious and maybe because, with little pain relief, he would have been in agony. Anything which enables him to forget his situation, would be useful to this soldier.

This poem demonstrates that, to the wounded soldier, something which reminds him of home and safety, can become of paramount importance. This is also demonstrated in *Stretcher Case* by Siegfried Sassoon, in which a wounded man, initially unsure of his whereabouts, arrives home by train and looks out of the window. He is relieved to discover that he is back in England. He knows this because he sees familiar sights, particularly advertisements for various items which he recognises. Such recognition makes his heart leap with happiness, because he now feels more safe and secure than he would have done had he not come home. In Gibson's poem, the soldier is trying to achieve this sense of security by chanting a rhyme which is familiar to him.

In the Ambulance was written at about the same time as *Breakfast* and, again, demonstrates Gibson's ability to capture the essence of a situation with minimal use of words. It also shows his unique capacity for understanding a situation of which he had little or no personal experience. He has managed to create a scene and an atmosphere which is completely believable, and all the more heart-rending for its lack of sentimentality.

LAMENT

Quite simply, this poem questions how those who survive the conflict can ever hope to regain a normal life, following the war, in the face of such overwhelming sacrifice.

In this simple, yet incredibly moving poem Gibson has captured a survivor's sense of guilt and, to a certain extent, shame, that he has survived while others have perished This is a fairly common sentiment, often found amongst the survivors of major conflicts or disasters. As ever, Gibson achieves this with an economic use of words, while still managing to convey his message to great effect.

Unlike much of his other work, *Lament* does not give the impression of having been written by a soldier-poet, but accurately portrays the poet as one who has been left out of the conflict, and as such this piece has something in common with some of the other 'home-front' poems, which were usually written either by women or non-combatants.

In this poem, Gibson is questioning how those who are left behind will ever be able to look upon the simple every-day things which they enjoyed in peacetime, while remembering the sacrifices which have been made on their behalf. Whilst he is probably pointing out that he feels this way himself, this poem could also be interpreted as a plea to others at home, to appreciate the human cost involved in gaining peace. Those who have died can no longer enjoy these simple pleasures. Gibson appears to be saying that if the survivors *truly* understand and appreciate the sacrifices being made, their lives can never have the same meaning again.

He seems to be elevating the dead soldiers to an exalted position, giving their dreams a righteous quality. This implies a sense of worthiness and value, yet he does this without glorifying their deaths. The final line demonstrates his acute sense of loss. He feels that *everything* in his life, right from its very core, will now be accompanied by an overwhelming sadness.

This is a poem of regret and gratitude. The deaths of so many soldiers are not seen here as glorious. *Lament*, in that sense, is dissimilar to some of the 'home-front' poems, which attempt to claim that the slaughter can be, in some way, justified. It is more reminiscent of, for example *The Fields of Flanders* by Edith Nesbit, or *Perhaps* by Vera Brittain.

In addition to his sense of gratitude and loss, Gibson demonstrates here that *he himself* is lost - as though he knows that the questions he is asking can never be answered. There is an element of desperation to find some sort of answer - to understand the waste and yet, underlying this, a realisation that this can never happen - it will never make sense. He seems to be asking for justification in continuing with his life, when others have not been allowed to do so.

This sad poem reflects Gibson's unhappiness at his non-combatant status. Written before he was finally accepted by the army, *Lament* demonstrates a feeling of guilt that Gibson could do nothing to further the war-effort himself. The heart-breaking realism of this poem makes his trench-life poems all the more impressive, especially when the reader realises that *Lament* was Gibson's reality while the rest came from his imagination.

JULIAN GRENFELL

BIOGRAPHY

Julian Henry Francis Grenfell was the eldest son of William and Ethel Grenfell. William Grenfell was, in fact, Lord Desborough and, had he lived, Julian would have inherited this title. Ethel (known universally as Ettie) was also an heiress, being descended from Earl Cowper and the Earl of Westmorland. Ethel had been orphaned at the age of three, which caused her to become, in adulthood, an unusually strong and independent woman. She also had an inclination towards mild flirtations with young men which, whilst tolerated by her husband, caused Julian much embarrassment.

Julian was born in London on 30th March 1888 and from the outset Ettie intended him for a career in the army. She was an extremely domineering mother who set high standards for all her five children. In an effort to please his mother and to avoid confrontation, Julian learnt very early in life not to show any emotion that wasn't directly linked to happiness. Such a bottling-up of any negative emotion is not healthy and led, later on, to great unhappiness.

Julian's formal education began at Summerfields Preparatory School in Oxford. At 13 years of age, he moved on to Eton and then in 1906 he went to Balliol College, Oxford. Separation from his mother caused confrontation between the two, with Julian attempting to exert his independence. His attitude to his mother may have been fuelled by the fact that her current "beau", Archie Gordon, was, at 20, only three years older than Julian.

Julian, always a loner, isolated himself from his Oxford friends and the the outcome of this and the conflict between mother and son was that Julian suffered a nervous breakdown. His family discreetly removed him from society and he was sent to recuperate with an aunt. Once recovered, Julian felt confident enough to form new friendships - even if his mother found his new acquaintances objectionable. He fell in love with Lady Victoria Marjorie Manners (known as Marjorie), but she rejected him in favour of Sir Charles Paget, 6th Marquess of Anglesey.

Dejected, Julian returned to Oxford and, although unable to concentrate on his prescribed studies of Classics and Philosophy, he launched himself into writing a series of essays which, essentially, were an assault on the standards and morals of English society. His mother and her entourage, at whom much of his writing was aimed, received these essays with contempt and his family ridiculed him.

Julian once again sank into depression in the autumn of 1909 upon the death of his mother's friend Archie Gordon, who was involved in a fatal car accident. Ettie's attention was focused on grieving for Archie and Julian's resentment of this led to another breakdown. This time he was sent to Italy to recover his health.

Returning to England the following summer, Julian embarked on a dangerous liaison of his own, becoming romantically and passionately involved with Pamela Lytton, who was married to the 2nd Earl of Lytton. Julian soon realised that this attachment had no prospect of success and that autumn decided to join the army. He was commissioned into the Royal Dragoons and posted, almost immediately to India. Always a keen sportsman, Julian spent his spare time in India playing polo, riding and hunting.

He was less than impressed, however, when his regiment was moved to South Africa in late 1911. During leave in late 1912, Julian approached Arthur Balfour, who had until recently been leader of the Conservative party, to enquire whether he might be able to stand for Parliament. Unable to decide which direction to take, Julian returned to his regiment in South Africa in April 1913. He once again sank into depression and by July 1914 had decided to leave the army and enter into politics. War was looming, however, and these ambitions had to be postponed when his regiment was sent back to Europe.

October 1914 found Julian in the Ypres Salient, where he appeared to relish the prospect of battle, writing of his happiness and saying that to him war seemed like a picnic. This "battle-cry" attitude has caused many critics to accuse Grenfell of being a warmonger. This is not necessarily the case, and even if true, this sentiment was quite common amongst his contemporaries. It should also be remembered that, although Grenfell was a professional soldier, this career path had been forced upon him by his family and was not of his choice.

One characteristic which Julian certainly did not lack was courage; he frequently ventured out of the trenches to snipe at unsuspecting Germans. He was twice mentioned in despatches and one of his escapades earned him the Distinguished Service Order (DSO). Early one November morning, Grenfell had crept out of his trench, hoping to spot some Germans. He spied a solitary German soldier who appeared from some woods. Grenfell shot him and a few minutes later several more German soldiers followed. From the level of noise, Grenfell sensed that many more Germans were concealed within the woods. Selecting, from those visible, the soldier who he felt looked most like an officer, Grenfell opened fire. He then rapidly retreated to his own trench, where he sent a message to the battalion on his right, informing them of the impending attack. The advance notice which this warning gave enabled the British to repulse the attack when it came. Julian was then offered the position of ADC (aide-de-camp - an officer who acted as a personal assistant to a more senior officer). He refused this less dangerous position, preferring to remain with his men.

He returned to England on leave in December and his family were naturally delighted to welcome their hero. Julian returned to France in January and in April enjoyed two days leave in Paris.

Back in the trenches, on April 22nd, the Germans used poison gas for the first time in the war, but failed to exploit the advantage which this new and deadly weapon had afforded them. The entry in Grenfell's diary for April 29th notes that he had written a poem entitled *Into Battle*.

By 13th May, the Royal Dragoons were in the second line trenches and Grenfell was acting as observer. While relaying messages, he was knocked down by a shell but was uninjured and continued with his duties. A little later there was another explosion near to him and a shell splinter became lodged in his skull. He was sent, via No. 10 Casualty Clearing Station, to hospital in Boulogne. He wrote a customarily cheery letter to his mother, stating that his skull was cracked, but he was doing splendidly. His sister, who was nursing at a nearby hospital, initially did not feel that his injuries were too serious. On May 16th, however, she sent a telegram to her parents urging them, if possible, to come to see Julian as soon as possible. Fearing the worst, his parents used their influence and obtained a passage on an ammunition boat the following day.

They were distraught at the prospect of Julian's death but despite their best efforts and two operations, he died on the afternoon of May 26th. Julian Grenfell's *Into Battle* first appeared in The Times on the same day as the announcement of his death.

Tragically, of the five Grenfell children, all three boys did not live to see their 30th birthdays. Julian's brother Gerald was killed in action on the 30th July 1915 at the age of 25. Ivo, who was ten years younger than Julian, died following a car accident on 8th October

1926. Thus, with the loss of all the male descendants, the Desborough line died out.

POETRY ANALYSIS

INTO BATTLE

This nature poem is, essentially, a celebration of life, the joy of fighting, and the honour of death, seen, by Grenfell, as a satisfactory fulfilment of man's existence.

This sense of joy is shown in the opening stanza, where the glory of a spring day is described. This can be contrasted with the later poems of, for example, Wilfred Owen, who even in his descriptions of this season in *Spring Offensive*, talks of the cold winds which prepare the men for battle.

Grenfell's language, on the other hand, in the first six lines of this poem, is gentle and cheery. The final two lines of the second stanza remind us of the war - changing the emphasis of the poem. It is Grenfell's belief that those who refuse to fight might as well be dead; and those who die fighting are the better for it: their lives are enriched and made more valuable by the manner of their death.

He re-iterates this in the third verse. He states here that men get their physical strength from nature - the sun, the earth, the winds all empower men and through the earth man is reborn. Death is not seen as the end, but as a coming-together between man and nature. In Owen's *Spring Offensive*, by contrast, men have turned their back on nature like an old friend or lover from the past. In *Into Battle* there is no futility - dying is a means to gain greatness and satisfaction.

Man is not merely linked with the earth. In the fourth stanza, Grenfell states man's connection with the stars and the heavens. His choice of these three constellations is interesting: the ancient

Egyptians believed that the Dog Star (Sirius), being so bright, was responsible for the summer heat; Orion, the hunter, famed for slaying wild animals, pursued the Seven Sisters (Pleiades) and upon his death, was placed as a constellation behind them, to continue the chase evermore. These constellations all represent strength - even the Seven Sisters, although pursued, are never caught.

Grenfell returns to earth in the following verse, this time to the trees. His trees are friendly - a guiding hand showing the men the way through the valley. In *Spring Offensive* Owen's valley, on the other hand, is full of unyielding brambles clutching and clinging to the advancing troops; his men are like unmoving trees - a much more sinister and threatening image of nature than the one painted by Grenfell.

Man's ability to blend and communicate with the earth is not limited to inanimate natural objects. In the sixth and seventh stanzas men and birds are linked. The kestrel and owl offer friendly warnings and endow men with their speed and good hunting senses. The blackbird, on the other hand, wisely bids man to enjoy his final hours - to seize the day - the singing is a metaphor for living; Grenfell is saying that if this coming battle is the last action you do on earth, fight well, for you may not get another chance.

The attitude of men in the hours of fear and boredom waiting for battle, when they tended to believe the worst, are contrasted with the noble courage of horses. It should be remembered that, as well as enjoying riding and hunting before the war, Grenfell was in the Royal Dragoons. He spent his First World War in the trenches, but his time in South Africa and India would have been largely spent on horseback.

In the ninth verse, the battle finally begins. To him it is a heated moment of joy, during which nothing else matters. His description of being taken by the throat and made blind could be an allusion to the poison gas which the Germans had employed for the first time only a few days before this poem was written.

The final two verses deal with the glory of death. The dying man doesn't much care about the manner of his death, whether it be by lead (bullet), or steel (bayonet). The battle is, again, likened to nature - this time the noise is described as being like thunder. The sounds of death coming from No Man's Land, which many would later describe as screams or cries, are compared by Grenfell with singing - thus giving the whole experience a musical and mystical quality. Finally he evinces the safety and sanctuary of death, which will wrap the dead in soft wings. The feeling this line evokes is one of purity and sanctity in death.

This poem was very popular at the time of its publication. Like Brook's *1914 Sonnets*, it promotes a gentle and heroic image of war. This was not untypical of much of the poetry being written at this time. Its publication, coming on the day of the announcement of Grenfell's death, made it even more poignant, as the author was now deemed to have made a noble sacrifice himself which, in the eyes of the public, further served to justify the content of his poem.

Hindsight is a wonderful tool with which we may look back and possibly deride this poem as unrealistic and a glorification of war. This would be unfair. Grenfell wrote what he felt. As with Rupert Brooke, who can say whether his tone would have changed had he lived longer.

IVOR GURNEY

BIOGRAPHY

It is often said that there is a fine line between genius and insanity, and this would certainly seem to have been true of Ivor Gurney. Although his training and much of his talent lay in musical composition, his poems demonstrate his heartfelt love for his home county and his fellow man. The realism and beauty of his poetry hides a troubled mind which the war would ultimately destroy.

Ivor Bertie Gurney was born on 28th August 1890 at 3 Queen Street in the city of Gloucester. He was the second child of David and Florence Gurney - his sister Winifred being three years older. When Ivor was only a few months old, the family moved to 19 Barton Street where his father, a tailor by trade, took a shop with living accommodation above. Florence Gurney (née Lugg) also helped in the family business. Ivor had two other siblings: Ronald born in 1894 and Dorothy in 1900.

Ivor's family, being down-to-earth, working-class people, found his artistic temperament difficult to understand. Fortunately, they had made for him an excellent choice of godfather - Canon Alfred Cheesman - who encouraged Ivor from an early age, nurturing his interests in music and literature. In addition to these subjects, Ivor also developed a love of the surrounding Gloucestershire countryside which would remain with him throughout his life. Ivor's musical talent showed itself quite early and at the age of twelve, he was invited to join the Cathedral Choir, as well as beginning full-time education at the city's King's School, where he was taught to play the piano as well as musical theory. He also enjoyed sports, such as cricket, football and hockey. His fellow pupils, however, found him eccentric and nicknamed him "Batty".

In 1906 he was articled to Dr. Brewer, the Cathedral's organist and remained under his tutelage until 1911. During this time he met two other young men from Gloucester who would become lifelong friends: Herbert Howells went on to become an award-winning composer and Frederick William Harvey (known as Will) became a poet during the First World War, and afterwards qualified as a solicitor. All three young men showed a passion for the English countryside and Harvey's family welcomed Ivor into their home, which allowed him, not only more intellectual and stimulating surroundings than he found with his own family, but also access to their piano, upon which he was always free to practice.

Ivor was awarded a scholarship in composition at the Royal College of Music in 1911, studying under Sir Charles Villiers Stanford who declared that, of all of his talented pupils, Ivor was among the finest and yet he was almost impossible to teach. In May of 1911 Ivor met Marion Scott who was editor of the college magazine and a music historian. She was also a champion of contemporary British music and composers, and would remain one of Ivor's truest friends for the rest of his life.

By 1914, Ivor had secured the position of organist at Christ Church in High Wycombe, which enabled him to escape from London at weekends, while continuing his studies during the week. At High Wycombe he was unofficially adopted by the churchwarden and his family. Edward and Matilda Chapman, to whom Ivor referred as "Le Comte" and "La Comtesse" had four children: Catherine (Kitty), Winifred (Winnie), Arthur and Marjorie (Micky) who ranged in ages from seventeen down to ten. Edward Chapman worked for the Great Western Railway as Chief Clerk to the Goods Manager at

Paddington. Ivor's weekend visits brought amusement to the Chapman children as they all enjoyed games of cricket and ping-pong with their guest, as well as joining him on long walks. He composed music on the piano in their drawing room and in the evenings he told humourous stories and tales of his beloved Gloucestershire, while sitting in front of the fire.

As Ivor spent more time with the Chapmans, his feelings for the eldest daughter, Kitty, developed into love. He sought Mr Chapman's permission to ask for her hand in marriage, but was told, very kindly, that Kitty - who was then just 17 years old - was too young to enter into an engagement. Despite his disappointment, Ivor's attitude to Kitty always remained friendly. When war was declared in August 1914, Ivor interrupted his studies and immediately tried to enlist. Initially he was rejected due to his poor eyesight. However, by 1915 the Army had lowered the standard of physical requirements, so he tried again and was accepted into the ranks of the 2nd/5th Gloucester Regiment.

Ivor's mental instabilities had already become apparent by this time, and although they only appeared as mild eccentricities, he was, nonetheless, disturbed by some of his own behaviour. He hoped that the rigours and discipline of army life would enable him to regain control of his mental faculties. His early letters, written both while in training and from the front, show that once he had joined up, there was a marked improvement in his mental condition.

Ivor's training took place in Northampton, Chelmsford, Epping Forest and Salisbury Plain, before he embarked for France, arriving at Le Havre on 26th May 1916. He wrote prolifically while in training and in France. As well as letters to his family, F.W. Harvey and, in particular, the Chapmans, he also wrote many poems. One of his greatest achievements while in France, was the setting to music of John Masefield's poem *By a Bierside* - a feat made remarkable by the fact that he had no access to musical instruments of any kind. Ivor sent all of his poems and compositions to Marion Scott who, having recognised his extraordinary talents, made copies of these and ensured their preservation. She also arranged for the publication of a volume of his poetry entitled *Severn and Somme* in 1917.

On Good Friday of 1917, Ivor was wounded in the arm and spent six weeks recovering at Rouen before returning to the trenches. That September, he was caught in a gas attack at Saint Julien which was sufficiently severe for him to be sent back to Britain, where he was admitted to Bangour War Hospital near Edinburgh. His recovery was aided by his nurse, Annie Drummond with whom he fell in love. By November, he was well enough to be discharged from hospital, but was still not considered sufficiently fit to return to France. He was posted instead to Seaton Delaval in Northumberland to attend a signalling course.

Ivor found life, both in the hospital and at the camp in Northumberland very difficult: he could not escape the feeling that he was somehow evading his responsibilities and also he deeply missed the comradeship of the trenches which had inspired him and given him solace, even in his darkest moments. By February 1918, Ivor was once again beginning to show signs of mental instability. He was hospitalised, initially at Newcastle-upon-Tyne and then County Durham. Although there were some signs of improvement, these were short-lived and by May he had been transferred to Lord Derby's War Hospital in Warrington, having suffered a complete breakdown. This was made worse by the ending of his relationship with Annie Drummond. She and Ivor had corresponded with each other since his departure from Edinburgh, but she now decided that she no longer wished to continue with this, causing Ivor to fall into utter, hopeless despair. He contemplated suicide, writing to Marion Scott that he would rather be thought of as dead than mad.

In July Ivor was transferred to the Middlesex War Hospital at
Napsbury in Hertfordshire, before being discharged from the army
in October due to 'delayed shell-shock. He was granted a pension
of twelve shillings per week - only half the normal allowance,
because it was deemed that although the war had aggravated his
mental condition, it had not been the root cause. He returned to
his parent's house in Gloucester, but his welcome there was an
uneasy one: his mother was pre-occupied with his father's health
(David Gurney was terminally ill and would die the following May),
and Ronald resented his brother's hospitalisation, seeing it as a form
of cowardice and avoidance of duty.

Once again, his family failed to understand him: his mind was in
turmoil and within a few days of returning home, Ivor decided to go
to sea. Luckily he was dissuaded from this course of action by the
opportune arrival of Edward Chapman who just happened to visit
Ivor on the same afternoon as he had decided to run away. Mr
Chapman was deeply concerned about Ivor's mental health and
during the course of the afternoon, he suggested to the Gurney's
that he and his wife should legally adopt Ivor. Mr and Mrs Gurney
refused this offer and Mr Chapman left that evening, still worried,
but slightly relieved by the knowledge that his visit had brought
about a noticeable improvement in Ivor's condition and he left him
much happier than he had found him.

This progress continued over the next few months, with the help of
his friends and long walks taken in his beloved Gloucestershire
countryside. In March 1919 he resumed his studies at the Royal
College of Music, under Ralph Vaughan Williams, and initially took
lodgings in London, although he eventually moved out to High
Wycombe. This move not only enabled him to play the organ at
Christ Church again, but also to meet regularly with the Chapmans.
He was happy and productive at this time and a second volume of
poetry was published under the title *War Embers*. Despite not living

in London, Ivor was also beginning to be recognised as a poet and composer and to mix with other literary figures, such as John Masefield, Robert Graves, Lascelles Abercrombie and Robert Nichols.

Just as his star was beginning to shine brighter than ever, the black, unpredictable hopelessness of depression once again descended. His behaviour became unpredictable and he spent less and less time at the Royal College of Music, took extremely long walks, often for days on end, and sometimes slept rough. The Chapmans became increasingly concerned for his welfare.

In the summer of 1921 he finally left the Royal College of Music and went to live with an aunt at Longford in Gloucestershire, undertaking a number of different jobs, ranging from farm worker to pianist at a cinema, but none of these lasted for more than a few weeks. His fears were becoming more irrational than ever - he believed he was being bombarded by radio waves and the voices in his head, which he had heard intermittently in the past, became more common and disturbing.

In September of 1922, Ivor moved, uninvited, into the home of his brother, Ronald, and his wife, Ethel. His eccentricity and behaviour became very erratic and he made several suicide attempts. Unable to tolerate this, and concerned for his welfare, Ivor's family had him committed to Barnwood House, a private asylum near Gloucester, where he was certified insane.

Ivor managed to escape from this institution, but was recaptured, so the decision was made that he should be moved away from Gloucestershire in order to lessen his desire for freedom. In December, he was transferred to the City of London Mental Hospital at Dartford in Kent. He also escaped from here, and went to visit Ralph Vaughan Williams, who reluctantly notified the authorities and Ivor was, once again, incarcerated.

Shortly after Ivor's removal from Gloucestershire, Mr Chapman was promoted to Goods Manager and transferred there, so the family moved into a house at the foot of Chosen Hill where Ivor had spent many happy hours walking. Mr Chapman visited Ivor at Dartford and his other visitors included Marion Scott and Helen Thomas - widow of poet Edward Thomas. On one of her visits, Helen took with her an Ordnance Survey map of some of Edward's favourite parts of Gloucestershire. She showed this to Ivor who delightedly traced footpaths with his fingers, while imagining and describing the joyous countryside which he could no longer enjoy, but which was still crystal clear in his mind's eye. Despite this, his mental condition continued to deteriorate, although this did not prevent him from writing and composing throughout most of his time at Dartford. He was occasionally allowed out on trips: Marion Scott, for example, occasionally took him to the Old Vic to see performances of Shakespeare's plays.

He found confinement intolerable and at times became hostile and abusive towards hospital staff. He was also delusional, believing himself to be - among others - Shakespeare and Beethoven. Ivor also wrote letters to the police, urging them to secure his release from imprisonment, so that he may either work, or be allowed to die in peace and freedom. This was a wish which was never granted: Ivor Gurney died in the mental hospital on 26th December 1937 from tuberculosis.

The letters which Ivor wrote to the Chapmans during and immediately after the war, give an enlightening insight into his personality. In these, he shows that he was always aware of his own mental fragility, yet he wrote very affectionate, kind and optimistic letters. Always self-effacing, the one quality which shines through is his sense of fun, particularly when writing to the Chapman children. He offered them encouragement in all their exploits and ambitions and frequently voiced his concerns over their ill-health. Another common trait is his praise for the courage, vitality and spirit of his fellow soldiers, while never seeking admiration for himself.

It has taken many years and a great deal of work by his friends and supporters, for Ivor Gurney's rare and joyous gifts to be fully appreciated - the most joyous of all, probably, being his warm heart, so full of humanity.

POETRY ANALYSIS

FIRST TIME IN

This poem begins by comparing the stories the men are told before going up to the front, with the reality that awaits them. The accounts of fighting are described as fearful and red, which presumably refers to the anticipated bloodshed, although Gurney's description gives these tales an air of mystery to a greater extent than if he had used more direct language. So, the men advance towards the front, uncertain of what they will find, and discover themselves sharing the trenches with a Welsh Regiment. The afterglow mentioned may refer to the fact that men often went up the line at sunset, but may also describe the lingering impression of comfort and peace which they discover when they reach their destination. The Welsh soldiers whisper quietly among themselves which enhances this sense of calm, although they appear to be speaking in a foreign language. This may be because they actually are speaking in Welsh, or because the things they are saying - such as descriptions of recent events - seem strange and unreal to these innocent, raw recruits.

Then Gurney describes how the new arrivals are taken into a dugout, with an oilsheet for a door which effectively shields them from the outside world. The Welsh soldiers welcome the newcomers warmly, making them feel more comfortable, even managing to make them feel like they are at home. They sing songs and in doing so they succeed in obliterating all other fears from the minds of the recent arrivals. The stories described so fearfully in the first line of the poem are now forgotten.

The next day, when the guns begin firing, one would expect this image of serenity to be banished and replaced by fear, but this is not the case. So warm has been the welcome that nothing can take away the memory of the previous evening. In fact, their fear itself has been dissipated by the kindness of their new friends. The description of war as a rout is interesting as this implies an overwhelming defeat which it would seem has been avoided by the considerate generosity of the Welshmen. The defeat in question here would not be in a battle, but the sense of impending doom and fear which may well have overwhelmed the men, and thus sapped their spirits.

The Welshmen share their meagre belongings and food, and Gurney seems to contrast this with the treatment received by Ulysses in Homer's Odyssey. Ulysses fought with the Greeks in the Trojan War and afterwards travelled back to his homeland, enduring many hardships along the way because he had angered the Gods. He received very little assistance during his journey because those he met were afraid to help him, in case the Gods became angry with them too.

Gurney remembers the traditional songs which the Welshmen sing, from lullabies and sad songs of farewell, to those sung in the mines. All of these are reminders of home and happier, more peaceful times, but have never seemed more wonderful than now, where death and fear surround them.

In this poem, written in 1916, Gurney creates a homely and surprisingly peaceful image of his first arrival in the trenches. His regiment, which sailed for France in May 1916, first went into the front line at Riez Bailleul, where they undertook a week's instruction with the London Welsh Regiment. This experience had a profound effect on Gurney, who later described it as one of the most amazing of his life. The simple kindness and homeliness of these Welshmen were exactly the introduction Ivor needed, as he tried to adapt to conditions in the front line. He had always hoped that through the discipline of army life, he would be able to control his mental instabilities and the calm atmosphere created here in the midst of the crashing war must have helped him. His appreciation and affection for these men is the overriding theme in this poem.

One poem which is worthy of comparison with *First Time In* is *Apologia Pro Poemate Meo* by Wilfred Owen, the title of which translates as "Reason for my poem". Owen's reason was to demonstrate that, despite the death, hatred and fear which surrounded him, he found cheerfulness and comradeship at the front, the like of which he had never experienced before. It is this spirit of humanity that he wishes to celebrate in this poem. His language is much more harsh than Gurney's, but Owen's poem was written, or at least begun, in November 1917, so his experience of the war was greater than Gurney's, who had not long arrived in France when he wrote *First Time In*. Owen also criticises those at home who seek to glory in the perceived cheerfulness of soldiers, believing it justifies their sacrifices and that they are happy to give up their lives. He points out that the attitude of the men is unique to them, and not something worthy of being shared with those who have no understanding of their suffering.

Although the language and tone of these two poems is markedly different, their messages are essentially the same: if you look for happiness you can find it, even in the most unlikely circumstances. Gurney's poem, with its lack of bitterness, illustrates that he (like many other soldiers) went into the war expecting the worst, but somehow hoping for a pleasant surprise. By opening himself up to the possibility of finding joy, it found him.

TO HIS LOVE

There is some confusion over the subject of this poem. Some anthologists maintain that it describes the aftermath of the death of F. W. Harvey, a close friend of Ivor Gurney. Harvey was reported as "missing, believed killed" in August 1916, although this was, in fact, inaccurate as he had been captured by the Germans and remained their prisoner until the end of the war. Although it is not clear when Gurney wrote this poem, it did not appear in print until 1919 when his second volume of poetry *War Embers* was published. By this time, he would have been aware that Harvey was still alive, so the subject is not necessarily him, but may have been another friend, or someone from Gurney's imagination.

The first two words sum up the depth and finality of Gurney's feelings. His friend is dead and he obviously deeply regrets his passing. He goes on to tell us that he can see no future as all the plans they made are of no value now. He remembers walks they used to take in the hills, but with the realisation that they will not do so again. Others, represented by the sheep, will carry on as before, able to ignore his pain at the loss of so dear a friend.

Next, he appears to discuss his feelings with another acquaintance who had been equally familiar with their friend's appearance. In doing so, he reminds us once again, that everything has changed. The dead man would be unrecognisable now, even to his greatest friends, although he seems to imply here that they should remember him as he was, rather than concentrating on what he has become.

Even though no amount of remembrance can alter the fact that his friend is dead, Gurney is proud of the fact that he died with honour and wants to commemorate this by covering his grave with a carpet of violets, reminiscent of his beloved Gloucestershire countryside.

This gives the impression that there will be some kind of memorial or funeral service, which, of course, cannot be. The final verse begins in an almost panic-stricken tone, as though Gurney himself has suddenly realised that the dead will remain unburied. He wants the body hidden from sight, covered with flowers which will shield the living from the memory of the man's wounds, and remind them of happier times. By referring to his body as a 'thing', Gurney is not necessarily just being imprecise, but he is reminding us that not all bodies, whether those of friends or enemies, were recognisable after death. The colour of the 'thing' and its wetness suggest that the wounds are fresh, and yet it would seem he is unable to identify exactly what it is he is looking at. He is also reminding us how difficult it will be for him to forget these hideous sights and this contrasts with his earlier happy memories of his friend while he was still alive.

It is the end of this poem which makes some anthologists believe he could not have been writing about F. W. Harvey as he would not have seen a body or its wounds. This does not, however, prevent him from imagining such things.

To His Love is a poem of remembrance - both of the life of a dead friend, and of home and more hopeful days. The "Love" of the title is not necessarily a homo-erotic reference, but is more likely to concern his feelings for the English countryside which the dead man can no longer enjoy. This poem celebrates human friendships, but also points out how difficult it is to witness the horrors of war and remain untouched by them.

Another poet who shared Ivor Gurney's love of the English countryside was Edward Thomas. He demonstrated this in many of his poems. In *The Cherry Trees* and *In Memoriam (Easter 1915)*, Thomas speaks of various elements of country life, particularly those surrounding the changing seasons and flowers, which the dead will no longer be able to experience. All of Thomas' poems were written before his departure for France, which accounts for the more pastoral air to his work. This is a tone which Gurney includes within *To His Love*, while providing a greater contrast between this and the horror of the war.

THE BOHEMIANS

This poem describes and outlines the some of the various types of people who served during the war, beginning with the ones who refuse to abide by the 'rules'. These men take little interest in their appearance, preferring comfort to regimental perfection. Putties, for example, were long pieces of material strapped around the lower leg, over one's trousers. If tied properly they looked neat and tidy, but the ends could easily be left hanging down if care was not taken. To disobey army regulations regarding appearance may have been interpreted by the more diligent officers as insubordination, which would have been a punishable offence. These men, however, are described as being barely able to adhere to the rules - they are not just unwilling.

They smoke and play cards, joking around in the trenches while others, who obey the rules, earn promotions. There is another group who continually debate whether the army is right or wrong. All the while, however, the men are changing, probably becoming more embittered and less caring in the process. Some of the men become officers, some are killed and yet none of them ever held an ambition to join the army - these are not professional soldiers.

Gurney demonstrates the equality of the war when he tells us at the end of this poem that, regardless of habits, rank, humour or cleanliness, they are all buried together in the earth of northern France. The army regulations are of no importance to them now.

The title of this poem is interesting. A bohemian is a person who disregards conventional standards of behaviour, either in manners or in appearance. At the time of the First World War, many artists, literary figures and intellectuals had a bohemian life-style. Gurney could therefore be implying that those who flout the regulations are the more intelligent, or at least more thoughtful, group of men.

Like many, Gurney disliked the war, especially as it seemed to achieve so little, yet he considered that it was a job that had to be done. Here he takes a slightly humourous look at army life - questioning the sanity of all the rules and implying that those who looked the smartest were the ones who gained promotions, regardless of their ability.

In his letters he points out that the things which keep a soldiers' spirits up are letters and parcels from home and the comradeship of the other men. The cleanliness of a soldiers' buttons has very little to do with his capacity to fight, or die, for that matter. The army response to this argument would, of course, be that the regulations helped to maintain discipline which is particularly essential at times of war. Gurney's viewpoint is probably a better reflection of reality - as seen from the perspective of the soldier in the trenches.

THE TARGET

This poem begins by describing the inevitability of killing in a war. Gurney points out that, when faced with the prospect of being killed, all men would strike first, in self-defence. He goes on to say that his mother is very afraid for his safety and implies that this fear is dominating her life. He is not necessarily referring to his own mother here, but mothers in general. His solution to this problem seems drastic, however, since although his death would stop his mother from worrying about his fate, it could hardly be argued that her position would be improved by this situation. He is trying to say here that sometimes one's fears are worse than reality: that death itself is not as frightening as the thought of dying.

Then he remembers the man he has just shot and wonders about his background, for example, whether he had any siblings - this obviously makes him think about who will be mourning this young man. Although initially he believed he had done the right thing in killing this man, he now begins to doubt this, looking to God for advice and receiving none. He decides that if he gets killed, he will find the man he shot and try to find out whether the physical pain involved in being killed is worse than the mental anguish of becoming a killer.

Finally it becomes clear that, to Gurney, this is madness: killing has become his job, since he must either do this or be killed himself. Despite all the grief and pain that follows, however, nothing changes. This is a world where God has ceased to take any interest in the follies of mankind.

The target of the title refers not only to the men Gurney must shoot, but also to himself: they are all targets. This enhances the atmosphere of madness in this poem, forcing the reader to question how it is possible for *everyone* to be a target at the same time. Gurney also seems to want justification for his actions, while realising that there is none. In suggesting that one solution to his problems would be his own death, he is making a shocking statement. Although he implies that his death would solve his mother's problems, one could also interpret this idea as a solution to his own difficulties: he would no longer need to worry about right and wrong and may even be able to find some answers.

He obviously feels that God has forsaken him - not only is there such horrendous suffering all around him, but God no longer listens to anything - cries, questions, pleas, worries - all go unheeded.

This poem demonstrates that Gurney did not hate his enemy - like many soldiers his feelings towards the Germans were more sympathetic - both sets of men were going through the same experiences. This shared existence brought about a natural understanding between people who were supposed to hate each other, and yet, in many cases, found that impossible. This is a theme which is touched upon in *Journey's End* by R C Sherriff. During a conversation with Raleigh, Osborne relates the story of a rescue party who had gone out into No Man's Land to bring back a wounded man. A German officer, in his trench, saw them trying to drag this man back in the semi-darkness, stood up and shouted out that they should carry him, firing lights into the sky so they could see what they were doing. The point of this story and, at least in part, *The Target*, is that these men were all human beings, with the same fears and feelings, being asked to behave in an inhuman manner towards other men who were in exactly the same position. As Gurney points out in the last line of this poem: how much more shambolic could the situation be?

He is also unsure whether it is worse to kill another person or be killed oneself, which shows a sense of guilt at taking another life. These feelings of guilt and confusion were fairly common themes in

First World War poetry. For example Wilfrid Wilson Gibson wrote, in his poem *Back*, of feeling guilty for killing other men. This is interesting, since Gibson never served in the trenches, so that he would seem to be implying here that the war, and all the pain and suffering that went with it, is *mankind's* fault - everyone is to blame. Siegfried Sassoon explored the idea of sympathising with the enemy in his poem *Reconciliation*, which is addressed to the mother of a dead soldier. Here he points out that German mothers are experiencing the same grief as British ones - the suffering is universal.

E. A. MACKINTOSH

BIOGRAPHY

Ewart Alan Mackintosh was born on 4th March 1893 in Brighton, Sussex. Despite the quintessential Englishness of his birthplace, his ancestry was Scottish, his father, Alexander, having originated from the Scottish Highlands. Alan, as he was referred to from an early age, was the child of a second marriage. His father's first wife had died, and he had subsequently married Alan's mother Lilian. Alan had one half-brother and four sisters and half-sisters. Alan's father worked as a Senior Official Receiver and they lived, with a governess and four servants in a Regency house in Brighton.

From the age of eleven Mackintosh attended Brighton College and quickly became interested in English and Classics. He joined the debating society, but although he was a keen participant, his arguments never brought him much attention. Academically he was a gifted student, but his prowess did not extend to the sports field. Unlike many schoolboys of his era, he disliked sports intensely.

In 1910, Mackintosh moved to St Paul's School in London, where he became editor of the school magazine. He also wrote poetry and acted in school drama productions. His extra-curricular activities dominated his time at school, much to the antagonism of his schoolmasters, who, naturally, wished that he would show as much interest and dedication towards his formal studies. Mackintosh, without being at all arrogant, knew just how much work he needed to do and the rest of his time was devoted to more pleasurable pursuits. He was extremely popular with his fellow students, who appreciated his lively sense of humour.

In 1912 he won a Classics scholarship to Christ Church Oxford and while there, he began to take a keen interest in his Scottish ancestry. He learned to speak Gaelic and play the bagpipes. He continued to write poetry and it is here that there lies a clue as to a possible romantic interlude. His Oxford poems tell of an initial infatuation, which developed and blossomed into love. Eventually, for reasons not specified, the tone of his poems changes and it becomes clear that this romance has ended.

Upon the outbreak of the First World War in 1914, Mackintosh left Oxford and enlisted. He was commissioned into the Seaforth Highlanders and sent to Golspie in the far north of Scotland. There was a special camaraderie in his regiment which had been formed by the Duke of Sutherland and many of the men within its ranks had worked on the Duke's estate. Mackintosh enjoyed this atmosphere of friendship, but felt less inclined towards the harsh disciplines of army life.

Finally, the Seaforths moved south, to Bedford, for training and, eventually, in July 1915, they embarked for France. Mackintosh, initially, felt very homesick but he kept his feelings to himself, only revealing his true sentiments in his poetry. He was popular amongst both officers and men and became Battalion Bombing Officer.

In September 1915, Mackintosh experienced a battle and real fear for the first time, at La Boisselle. He survived unscathed and returned home for a short period of leave. Winter back in the trenches was a harsh experience, but Mackintosh found ways of keeping the men and his fellow officers cheerful. He discovered a natural talent for writing comic alternative versions of popular songs, which he performed at impromptu concerts.

March 1916 found Mackintosh just north of Arras. The trenches in this sector were terrible, having been dug-in over previous battlegrounds, unearthing bodies from earlier battles. As the

Bombing Officer, he was in great demand for raiding parties. One such raid took place on May 16th. Mackintosh and Second Lieutenant Mackay led a party of men into the German trenches. Many Germans were killed and five dugouts were bombed. A nineteen year-old private, named David Sutherland, was badly wounded and Mackintosh picked him up and carried him for some time, until it became clear that the young soldier was dead. Reluctantly, Mackintosh had to leave his body behind, in order to help others get back. Four of his men were killed and twelve wounded. This episode was the inspiration behind his poem *In Memoriam* and his courage on that day earned him a Military Cross. His citation, which appeared in the London Gazette on 24th June 1916 read:

"For conspicuous gallantry. He organised and led a successful raid on the enemy's trenches with great skill and courage. Several of the enemy were disposed of and a strongpoint destroyed. He also brought back two wounded men under heavy fire."

In July, after several other moves along the front, Mackintosh and his men were involved in an attack at High Wood. During this battle, he was badly gassed and returned to England to recover. It was a slow process of recuperation, taking six months, during which time as the casualty lists continued to grow, he became more and more overcome by feelings of guilt that he was safe while his men were still facing death. Like many soldiers he found home life difficult. Communicating with civilians was almost impossible and he marvelled at their lack of understanding. It was at this time that he wrote *Recruiting*, which was his response to the attitude that he encountered in England.

Once Mackintosh had been declared fit, he was posted to the Officer Cadet Battalion in Cambridge, where he passed on his bombing skills and experience to young officers in training. While stationed in Cambridge, he met and fell in love with a young doctor named Sylvia Marsh and they made plans to marry. Mackintosh was, however, still plagued by feelings of guilt which were exacerbated by the death of a close friend in August 1917. Finally, he could bear it no longer, and he volunteered to return to France. Although he knew he would miss Sylvia, he hoped that she would understand his feelings and forgive him. He returned to France at the end of September.

Ewart Alan Mackintosh was killed less than two months later, on the second day of the Battle of Cambrai, November 21st 1917. He is buried at Orival Wood Cemetery at nearby Flesquieres.

Just one month before his death, Mackintosh wrote a poem entitled *To Sylvia* in which he asks his beloved to forgive him and explains his sense of inner peace now that he is back with his men. He describes how he had felt that, by remaining safe, he was betraying his dead friends, but that now he is back in France, he has been able to regain his pride.

Mackintosh's poetry, above all, displays this sense of belonging, his pride and his courage. It also reflects an officer who respected, loved and cared for his men. These were feelings which, given the nature of Ewart Alan Mackintosh, his men could do nothing but return.

POETRY ANALYSIS

IN MEMORIAM

(Private D Sutherland killed in action in the German trench, May 16th 1916, and the others who died)

This poem demonstrates the strength of the relationship between an officer and his men. It is initially addressed to Private Sutherland's father, but in the final two verses, Mackintosh speaks directly to his men. The poem tells of the comparative innocence of the men when they left home and how they now look to their officer for protection and comfort in the absence of their fathers. It also describes the officer's intense feelings towards his men and his desire to protect them.

In Memoriam is a very moving poem, which above all, shows the deep affection which Mackintosh felt for his men. In addressing this poem to David's father, Mackintosh makes himself into a father-figure which was a common feeling amongst good officers, who often had a profound sense of responsibility towards the men who served with them.

Mackintosh reiterates this by saying that he has more than one son - he is a father to all of his men. He hadn't known them as babies, or while they were growing up but they turn to him now, in their final moments, for comfort. He may not have brought them into the world, but he is the one who must take care of them when they are leaving it.

He appears to feel guilty that he has been unable to really assist, or save, his men and has to watch helplessly while they die, crying out for him. One senses his torment at his own incapacity, yet, knowing what a well-loved and respected officer he was, one cannot help but feel he is being too harsh on himself.

He remembers David's letters to his father, which, as an officer, he would have had to censor. These letters, he recalls, spoke only of matters relating to David's life at home, not mentioning the war at all. This reminds us that many soldiers did not want to worry their relations, and so refrained from mentioning their own situation. Mackintosh, however, would have had to write very different letters - informing parents that their sons had been killed. This poem paints a very realistic picture of battle and its awful consequences, but also shows Mackintosh's appreciation of the grief suffered by those at home when they received such a letter telling of the death of a loved-one. His image of the father, who can no longer function properly since David's death, helps to demonstrate his own depth of feeling and understanding. As the officer in charge, Mackintosh would have no time for such demonstrations of grief himself, yet he can understand the need for it in others. He must carry on and care for his remaining 'sons'.

His reference to the beauty and strength of his men does not necessarily have any homo-erotic connotations. It must be remembered that Mackintosh was writing about his men as though he were there father, or at least their guardian and protector, so his appreciation of their physique would have been, if anything, paternal.

Mackintosh obviously feels responsible, particularly for David's death and almost certainly for leaving his body behind. He regrets the fact that the Germans have David's body, yet makes no mention of his own heroics. We know from his Military Cross citation that he brought two wounded men back through heavy fire but he does not refer to this. The men he has saved seem of less importance than his feelings of inadequacy over the loss of one life.

This sense of responsibility for the men under an officer's command is demonstrated in many other poems. Examples of this include *Banishment* by Siegfried Sassoon, *Apologia Pro Poemate Meo* by

Wilfred Owen and *Comrades: An Episode* by Robert Nichols. This latter poem, in particular, deals with an officer's affection for his men and tells how, although wounded and stranded in No Man's Land, the officer's wish to see his men again before he dies forces him to find the strength to drag himself back to his own trench. However, upon reaching the trench, two of his men are shot and killed while trying to help him. The officer is overcome by grief and dies calling out for his men. Again, as in Mackintosh's poem, Nichols' officer demonstrates a sense of love for his men which is stronger than any bond of family. Although the officer, while dying, has fleeting thoughts of home, his overriding emotions are directed towards those with whom he has served.

Another poem, along similar lines, also written by Mackintosh, is entitled *Farewell*. In this poem, he is saying goodbye to dead comrades with fondness and looking back on the memories they all shared. Again, he makes it clear that, regardless of rank, he had very strong feelings for the men with whom he shared his war.

Mackintosh's poems give the impression that the bond he has been able to forge and the happiness he has discovered in the trenches, whilst in themselves, not uncommon, have given him a sense of pride and justification. He does not speak of hatred for the enemy, patriotism or glory; just love.

RECRUITING

The first section of this poem is an ironic look at the posters, patriotic newspaper reporting, jingoistic verse and generally complacent attitude of those at home, who willingly goad others to fight, while being neither prepared nor called upon to do so themselves. Mackintosh ironically suggests that these 'calls to arms' should be more realistic: they should point out that these men will increase the casualty lists and fill the newspaper columns with news of their deaths and injuries. However, according to his interpretation of the civilian viewpoint, provided that the Germans are kept at bay, it matters not how many men must die.

Mackintosh uses satire to show how he feels about these civilians and their messages, comparing their fictional interpretation of the conflict with the reality which he knows, though bitter experience, to be true. This leads into the second half of the poem, where Mackintosh presents his view of a more realistic war. Yes, it's cold, it's uncomfortable and you'll probably die, he says, but you'll die surrounded by some of the best men you'll ever meet.

He suggests that men should come, not for any patriotic or nationalistic reason, but to learn what magnificent people their fellow soldiers will be. They should forget all the warmongering at home, he says, and discover their own inner strength amongst true friends, sharing harsh experiences.

He paints a picture of happy comradeship, while never attempting to shield these potential soldiers from the certainty that they will die. The sacrifice which those at home uphold as so virtuous, is anything but, yet it is at least an honest, honourable and brave way to die, unlike the civilians who suggest they go, while remaining in safety themselves.

Finally, in the very last line of the poem, Mackintosh implores the men to join him, and die. He puts this bluntly, but the realism in these closing three words demonstrates that he genuinely believes men are better off facing the realities of the front - no irony, no satire - just the brutal truth of death.

This poem was written after Mackintosh had been at home convalescing for some time, and his anger at civilians is well demonstrated. This is a theme which is often repeated in First World War literature. In *Birdsong* by Sebastian Faulks, for example, Michael Weir returns home on leave and becomes uncontrollably angry at the attitude which he encounters in England, even in his own family. Many poets also used this theme, most notably, Siegfried Sassoon who frequently wrote using quite shocking language and great irony to demonstrate his anger and bitterness - *The Glory of Women* is a good example of this.

Mackintosh's message is slightly different from Sassoon's however. Where Sassoon shows bitterness, Mackintosh shows pride. To Sassoon these men's deaths were a waste, while to Mackintosh their courage in facing death is worthy of celebration. Like Robert Nichols, Mackintosh shows his feelings of pride and gratitude towards his fellow men and officers; and demonstrates his sense of comradeship which is greater and more important than any glorious sacrifice or worthy cause.

This poem also shows how he, in fact, longed to return to his men at the front. Like the character John Hilliard in Susan Hill's *Strange Meeting*, it would seem that Mackintosh felt more at home in the trenches than in England. He describes his fellow soldiers in glowing terms, while vehemently criticising those at home.

Many question whether this poem is pro-war or anti-war. The answer is - probably neither. Although the poet is suggesting that men should join the fight, this is not done in a jingoistic manner - in fact he is criticising those who use such language, but he is not critical of the war in itself. He does not suggest that men should fight for King and Country or even to keep their families safe from the Germans. His reason is that he wants them, like him, to discover true comradeship, and the strength of feeling that is possible between people who share experiences such as theirs.

While he is, naturally, angry at the civilians, he does not have a political axe to grind; he is not questioning the justification of the war itself - this does not concern him. Instead he is saying to young men that all the nationalist fervour at home is empty and full of insincerity. The reality is much harsher, with death and hardship as constant and unquestioned companions. But, he seems to say, all of this is worthwhile because of the quality of the men with whom one serves, and dies. These are better men than those who stay at home, urging others to protect them.

Staying in England with such people had, by this stage, become intolerable to Mackintosh whose pride, love and respect for his fellow soldiers dominates this poem.

JOHN MCCRAE

BIOGRAPHY

John McCrae was born on 30th November 1872 at Guelph, Ontario in Canada. He was the second son of Lieutenant General David McCrae of the Field Artillery, and his wife Janet Simpson Eckford McCrae. John's paternal grandparents had emigrated from Scotland in 1849, and the family retained a strong affinity with Britain. Religion played an important role in John's upbringing and this was coupled with a fervent interest in literature. He was also very keen on the military.

John's early education took place at the Central Public School and then at Guelph Collegiate Institute. It was during his time at the Institute that John took his first steps into the military, when he joined the Highland Cadet Corps at the age of fourteen. A year later, he became a bugler in his father's regiment of the artillery. Academically, he was a high achiever and when he was sixteen years old, he became the first student from his town to be awarded a scholarship at the University of Toronto.

John proved to be an excellent and popular student until in 1892, ill health forced him to take a year's leave of absence from university. In fact the recurring asthma which caused this temporary break in his education, would plague him, intermittently, for the rest of his life. During this year, he worked at the Ontario Agricultural College, teaching mathematics and English. This was to prove a difficult and unhappy time for John, who did not take naturally to teaching at this stage of his life. He also had his first, unhappy, experience of love, when he met, and formed an attachment to, the eighteen year-old sister of one of his friends. Tragically, she died shortly afterwards. When John returned to Toronto in 1893, he was relieved to leave this troubled time behind him, and resume his studies.

John completed his BA in Natural Sciences before commencing his medical training. He qualified as a doctor in 1898 at the age of twenty-six, graduating at the top of his class. He become resident house officer at the Toronto General Hospital and then, the following year, he moved to Baltimore in Maryland to join his older brother, Thomas, at the Johns Hopkins Hospital.

Later in 1899, McCrae was awarded a fellowship in Pathology at McGill University in Montreal. However, he decided to postpone taking up this position when Great Britain became involved in the Boer War that October. McCrae enlisted in December 1899 and was commissioned into D Battery of the Royal Canadian Artillery. He sailed for South Africa on January 20th 1900, landing in Cape Town. McCrae was caught up in the perceived excitement of his new situation and this feeling was enhanced by his meeting with one of his literary heroes, Rudyard Kipling.

During his time in South Africa, McCrae was involved in some fierce fighting, and also visited a military hospital, where he was quite shocked at the appalling conditions in which the men were being treated. In January 1901, having been promoted to Captain, McCrae and his unit returned to Canada, where he received praise for his qualities of leadership and his good conduct. In 1902, he was again promoted and now bore the rank of Major. He resigned his commission in 1904 and, it is said, rarely spoke of his experiences in South Africa, although he did write some poems which were set during that time.

Meanwhile, he had returned to McGill University to resume his previously postponed fellowship and became a respected lecturer on bacteriology and pathology. Following a year of studying in Britain, in order to gain his qualifications from the Royal College of Physicians, McCrae set up practice in Montreal in 1905.

He was a gregarious man, with a good sense of humour, who was well thought of by his friends. In 1908, he was appointed Physician to the Royal Alexandra Hospital for Infectious Diseases. His reputation as a thoroughly professional lecturer and physician continued to flourish. However, success in his professional field was not mirrored in his personal life. Despite several romances, this eligible bachelor never married.

McCrae frequently travelled to Europe, and was on board a ship, bound for England, when the First World War was declared. Canada swiftly followed Britain in declaring war on Germany and McCrae sent home a telegram offering his services to the Canadian Forces, either as doctor, or artillery officer. He sailed back to Canada at the end of August, but at the age of 41, was deemed too old to re-enlist. Nonetheless, his talents were too good to refuse and he was appointed Brigade Surgeon with the rank of Major.

On 3rd October 1914, he set sail again for England, taking with him a gift from a friend - a horse named Bonfire. He spent several months in training on a cold Salisbury Plain before embarking for France in February 1915, where he took part in the Battle of Neuve Chapelle between 10th and 13th March. McCrae acted as both physician and artillery officer, issuing orders to men and also looking after their health and welfare issues, as well as tending to the wounded in his dressing station

In April 1915, his unit moved into the Ypres Salient, just in time for the Germans to unleash their newest weapon - chlorine gas. He saw action during the Second Battle of Ypres, during which over 60% of the Canadian troops involved were either killed or wounded.

On 2nd May, one of McCrae's close friends, Lieutenant Alex Helmer was hit by a shell and killed. In the absence of a chaplain, McCrae took charge of the hastily convened funeral service and Helmer was buried in a make-shift grave just behind the lines. Wild poppies were beginning to flower between the growing number of wooden crosses, and it is thought that this sight and the feelings he experienced, provided McCrae with the inspiration for his poem *In Flanders Fields*, which was reputedly written the following day.

The fighting continued into the summer, and as the casualty rate grew, McCrae found himself transferred to the Canadian Army Medical Corps, where his skills as a physician were becoming more necessary. He was promoted to Lieutenant-Colonel and became Chief of Medical Services at Number 3 Canadian General Hospital at Dannes-Camiers near Boulogne. That October, the hospital was forced to move when the tents in which it was housed were badly damaged by storms. McCrae now found himself stationed at the Jesuit College in Boulogne.

In Flanders Fields was published anonymously in *Punch* on 8th December 1915, and was an instant success. It touched the hearts of millions, with its message that the deaths of so many should not be allowed to happen in vain. The poem was translated into many languages and became particularly popular in America.

Such a long period of service in France was beginning to take its toll on McCrae. As well as the obvious exhaustion from treating so many wounded men, with very little sleep between shifts, McCrae also felt guilty that he was 'safe' behind the lines, while so many others were dying. After the Battle of the Somme, he was hospitalised at Wimereux, suffering from severe asthma attacks. He took some leave, travelling to England to stay with friends, but was back in France in time to treat the wounded from the Battle of Vimy Ridge in April 1917. This battle saw a great victory for the

Canadian forces, who took the ridge following two years of unsuccessful and costly attempts by both the French and the British. Their success was not achieved without great losses: over 3,500 Canadians were killed and nearly 11,000 wounded, so McCrae was kept very busy indeed.

There followed a summer and autumn of very heavy fighting at Passchendaele and, once again, McCrae's health faltered. By January 1918, following several bouts of bronchitis and asthma, he diagnosed himself as suffering from pneumonia. He was, once again, hospitalised at the Number 14, British General Hospital for Officers. On 24th January it was announced that McCrae had been awarded the position of Consulting Physician to the First British Army - the first time such an honour had been bestowed on a Canadian. Unfortunately, his health continued to deteriorate and four days later, on January 28th, at the age of forty-five, John McCrae died.

John McCrae was buried, with full military honours, at Wimereux Cemetery. His funeral was attended by an impressive list of senior officers, including General Sir Arthur William Currie, the Commander of Canadian Forces, fellow surgeons and over seventy-five nurses. In accordance with military tradition, the funeral procession was led by his horse, Bonfire, with his master's reversed boots in his stirrups.

McCrae, as a skilled and efficient medical man, obviously gave great service, both in peacetime and during two wars, but especially throughout his time in France. He demonstrated, however, that as well as being a remarkable physician, he was also a wonderful observer. He witnessed, and captured, a moment in time, and through the words of his immortal poem, gave us the enduring symbol by which we may still remember.

THE HISTORY OF THE POPPY APPEAL

On 9th November 1918, an American YMCA worker and teacher, Moina Michael, was working at the organisation's Overseas War Secretaries Headquarters. During her morning break, she picked up a copy of the *Ladies Home Journal* and, leafing through it, she came across a copy of the poem *In Flanders Fields* by John McCrae. Although she had read this poem before, on this occasion, Moina was particularly moved by its message. She jotted down a poetic response, entitled *We Shall Keep The Faith* in which she promises that those who died will continue to be honoured.

Later that same morning, Moina was presented with a cheque for $10 by delegates attending a conference in the building. She decided to use this money to buy twenty-five red poppies and give them out to the attending delegates. Moina considered that, because the money used to buy these poppies was a donation, she was responsible for the first sale of poppies to commemorate the dead of Flanders.

After the war, Moina campaigned to have the red poppy adopted in the United States as a symbol of remembrance. After a few disappointments, this was achieved at the National American Legion Convention in September 1920. This Convention was attended by Madame E. Guérin, who became known as 'The Poppy Lady from France'. She brought millions of artificial poppies with her from France and sold them to the Americans to raise money for the aid of children in the regions of France and Belgium which had been laid waste by the war.

In 1921, Madame Guérin sent French women to London to sell poppies and at the same time, she visited Earl Haig to attempt to persuade him to help with the adoption of the poppy as a symbol of remembrance in Great Britain. Douglas Haig had been Commander in Chief of the British Forces from December 1915 until the end of the war. In 1921 Haig used his influence to help amalgamate several veterans associations, thus forming the British Legion.

The first official Legion Poppy Day was on the 11th November 1921. In 1922, the Poppy Factory was established, its aim being to allow the disabled to manufacture poppies for the appeal. The Factory, at Richmond in Surrey, still exists and today, over 70% of the workers there are disabled or suffer from chronic illness. The British Legion was granted its 'Royal' designation in 1971 and now produces over 34 million poppies every year, raising annually in excess of £21 million. The symbol of the poppy is used across the world to commemorate the dead, and assist those affected by war.

This remarkable achievement is due to the hard work and dedication of many thousands of volunteers, who work tirelessly, year after year, to raise funds. In acknowledging their efforts, one must also remember the inspiration of fifteen lines of poetry, written in a very different world, nearly one hundred years ago, on a warm spring morning in 1915, by John McCrae.

POETRY ANALYSIS

IN FLANDERS FIELDS

This poem, originally entitled *We Shall Not Sleep*, has a simple message: that the sacrifices being made by so many should not be in vain, and that those who follow should continue to pursue the cause for which these men have died.

John McCrae has written this poem from the perspective of the dead, addressing the living. He speaks of all the things that the dead miss or will no longer be able to enjoy, and then pleads with the living, urging them to keep faith with the dead, in order that they may rest peacefully.

In the first verse, McCrae describes his whereabouts, making it clear that he is writing from the perspective of a fallen soldier, but also that the war continues around him, regardless of the flowers that grow, and the birds that sing. War, and therefore death, pay no attention to nature, and the killing goes on.

The second stanza expands on the first, but the tone is more remorseful. Here he expresses sorrow at the passing of unfulfilled lives and regret at lost opportunities. Finally, in the third verse, comes the appeal to the living, that they should pursue the cause so that the dead may finally rest.

The theme of this poem is fairly clear: that the dead deserve not to go unnoticed, and that the living have a continuing responsibility to carry on the fight. This latter sentiment has, over time, been diluted and re-interpreted as a plea that the living should not forget those who have died. It seems clear, however, that McCrae's intention was to demonstrate that the survivors should carry on the fight against the enemy. One of the reasons for this loss of meaning over the years, is that this third verse has often been omitted altogether. In the period following the end of the First World War, thoughts turned naturally towards peace and forgiveness and it was not necessarily prudent to remind the public of previous hostilities. What was considered decent patriotic sentiment in war-time, was not required reading when thoughts of peace and reconciliation were paramount.

McCrae's use of language in this poem is also interesting. He contrasts the larks singing with the overpowering cacophony of the guns; the crosses represent death, yet he stipulates that the dead are not yet even asleep. This implies that he does not perceive them as dead at all. He gives these nameless dead appealing characteristics to make us feel even more sympathy for them - he points out that all of them have been loved by someone and have given love in return. His reference to the dawn and the sunset implies birth and death, which are natural enough in the normal course of events, but in this instance, life has been snatched from these men before they have even had the opportunity to experience it to the full. The mentioning of dawn and/or sunset is frequently used by poets, such as Wilfred Owen in *Anthem for Doomed Youth*, Siegfried Sassoon in *Attack*, and, probably most famously of all, Laurence Binyon's *For The Fallen*.

The tone of *In Flanders Fields* is fairly typical of the time during which it was written. Julian Grenfell's *Into Battle* was written at the end of that April, while Rupert Brooke's *1914 Sonnets* were completed early in 1915 and published that June. There are some obvious similarities between these poets, as in, for example, their belief in the justness of the cause for which they were fighting. They all perceive, although possibly for different reasons, that to fight the war to its conclusion is the right and proper course of action. McCrae's assertion that the dead can only find true peace if others follow them, demonstrates a call to arms. This is possibly because he and his family had retained strong links with Britain and he felt, and had demonstrated, that his loyalties lay with The British Empire and all that it stood for.

The main difference between these poets is their perception of death. Brooke and Grenfell perceive death through battle as glorious - a worthy and fitting end. McCrae, on the other hand, sees death as a source of regret and sorrow.

Unlike many later poets, such as Owen and Sassoon, McCrae does not attach any sentiment of waste or futility to these deaths, *unless* those who remain do nothing. Whilst his message is very different from that of Sassoon, for example, these two poets share a loyalty towards the victims of the war. The difference between them is in their ideal solution: Sassoon wanted (and indeed tried) to end the fighting because he believed that Britain's war aims were unclear and that the lives of so many men were being needlessly wasted. McCrae, on the other hand, while regretting the losses, urges others to avenge them, by continuing the fight on their behalf.

McCrae's belief that the living should avenge and mourn the dead could also be contrasted with the attitude of Charles Hamilton Sorley in his poem *When You See Millions of the Mouthless Dead*. Sorley maintains that there is little point in mourning the dead. They have been claimed by death and as such cannot hear your words, see your tears or respond to your grief. Both poems were written early in 1915 but the difference in their content is so marked that the reader could easily believe Charles Hamilton Sorley was writing much later in the war.

In Flanders Fields captured the imagination of millions of people who were just beginning, like McCrae, to understand the cost of the First World War. His statement that these men should not go forgotten to their graves, coupled with a sense of empowering their survivors to continue the fight in their name, was at that time a stirring declaration. Whilst it is easy to look back with hindsight and the eyes of the 21st century and criticise such an imperialistic point of view, to do so would be unreasonable. The writing of poets such as McCrae, Brooke, Grenfell etc., must be judged, more fairly, on the basis of *their* lives and the world in which *they* lived.

THE ANXIOUS DEAD

The Anxious Dead is addressed to the guns, which McCrae bids to be quiet, just for a short while - long enough, at least, for the dead to hear that soldiers are still marching forwards. These dead, and buried soldiers have fought in a fearsome battle, but died without seeing its conclusion. This could imply a single battle, but more likely suggests the *whole* war, which obviously at this stage has no conclusion. McCrae intimates that this lack of knowledge of the outcome of the war greatly troubles the dead, and prevents them from resting peacefully.

In the second verse, McCrae repeats his request that the the guns should cease. Again though, this silence should not signify the end of the war, but should allow the dead to witness the dawn. In this way, they may realise that life goes on, and that despite so many deaths, there is still hope. Then the tone of the poem changes as he bids the guns to start up again, in a massive show of strength - all the guns blazing in unison, like an enormous, deadly choir. The noise created should be so vast that the dead - both First World War soldiers and, in fact, all warriors, right back to Caesar, would realise that the war is still being fought and that their lives have not been needlessly sacrificed.

The third verse urges the guns to continue firing, to let the dead know that the fight goes on and that the survivors will keep fighting until they either gain victory or are killed themselves.

In the final stanza, he says that the guns should tell the men to bide their time and wait. Then at some point in the future, there will, once again, be peace. He anticipates, however, that this is going to take some time to achieve, but when it does happen, the dead will witness one final tranquil dawn before finally being allowed to sleep peacefully forever.

The first point of interest in analysing this poem is the title. The dead are anxious, not sad, peaceful, glorious, betrayed or embittered. McCrae portrays them as unable to rest because they are worried about the outcome of the war. He had used this same theme in his earlier poem *In Flanders Fields*. For the families of the dead soldiers, one of the few minor consolations was that the dead could now be at peace. McCrae is attempting in both of these poems to destroy that myth. The dead, he says, are not yet able to rest properly because the war is not yet won.

He addresses his poem to the guns, which is not altogether surprising as he had been an artillery officer. A poem along similar lines is Rupert Brooke's *The Dead (I)* from his *1914 Sonnets*. Brooke, however, addresses himself to bugles and his dead have been made honourable and glorious by death. This contrasts with McCrae's impression that death achieves nothing for the victim: it is victory that buys peace for both the living and the dead.

This poem was published in the summer of 1917, over two years after *In Flanders Fields* first appeared, yet the two poems have a remarkably similar message. That is, that the victims of the war should not be allowed to have died in vain and the survivors have a responsibility to continue the fight. The fact that the meaning of these two poems is so similar, despite the passage of time, implies a stalemate: for McCrae it would seem that nothing has changed since May 1915 and he still feels it necessary to urge others to continue to fight.

This is unusual since most poets who were writing in this style in 1915, had, by 1917 completely revised their viewpoint. A good example of this can be seen in the work of Siegfried Sassoon. In 1915, in his poem *Absolution*, Sassoon tells us that fighting for freedom is more important than any losses that must be endured along the way. By the end of 1916, however he had written *The Poet as Hero* in which he tells us that he now sees the war as wasteful rather than glorious and attempts to explain his change of heart. Even here, however, he speaks of his desire to avenge his dead friends. Summer 1917 saw Sassoon writing in his more familiar style, in poems such as *Lamentations*. His extremely ironic tone here suggests that men should display their patriotism by not grieving openly for the dead.

The language used in *The Anxious Dead* is also noteworthy. McCrae makes a connection between verses one and two by referring to Caesar and legions of men. This implies that these are no ordinary soldiers, but a conquering army. This element of 'death or glory' is reiterated in the third verse where he suggests that the only possible outcomes for the living soldiers are to perish or to be victorious. Defeat is not even worthy of consideration. Also in verse three, he suggests that the soldiers march onward, which brings to mind the hymn *Onward Christian Soldiers*, which was written in 1865 and would have fitted in well with McCrae's religious background. Once again he echoes the sentiment in the last line of verse three, that men should keep the faith. The faith in this instance is not a religion, but refers to the reason *why* the soldiers have died - more a sense of brotherhood with the dead. This is a theme he has repeated from *In Flanders Fields*.

In the final verse, McCrae mentions the dawn which traditionally symbolises birth. In this instance, however, because the dawn is finally quiet, this means that the dead may rest peacefully. This implies that McCrae believes that the dead have paid the price in order for everyone to enjoy a new, peaceful dawn and their reward is to sleep for eternity. The rebirth of the world will happen without them, but they have sacrificed themselves in order to achieve it.

Although it can seem difficult to equate McCrae's position as a physician with his poetry which seems to be a call to arms - and therefore, by extension, a call to potential death, it must be appreciated that he believed firmly in the justness of Britain's cause at that time. Many others disagreed with his sentiments, but there is no doubt that he had a deep sense of gratitude and respect for those who had sacrificed so much.

ROBERT NICHOLS

BIOGRAPHY

Robert Malise Bowyer Nichols was born in the autumn of 1893 in Shanklin on the Isle of Wight. He and his younger brother and sister, (Philip and Irene) had a socially privileged childhood which was, unfortunately, overshadowed by the mental instability of their mother, Catherine. Robert's father, John, was an artist and journalist. Following Robert's education at Winchester and Trinity College, Oxford, Nichols came into contact, and became friends, with many of the best known literary figures of the time.

Upon the outbreak of the First World War, 21 year old Nichols was commissioned as a Second Lieutenant in the 104th Brigade of the Royal Field Artillery. Following training he was sent to France in August 1915, taking part in the Battle of Loos the following month. His service at the front was short, however, and by August 1916 he had been invalided out of the army, suffering from shell-shock. During his recovery he was treated by Henry Head, a colleague of Dr W. H. R. Rivers, who, famously, treated Siegfried Sassoon at Craiglockhart War Hospital.

Nichols, in 1918, joined the British Mission (Ministry of Information), and travelled to America, giving lectures on poetry.

During the First World War, he had become friends with several other war poets. In January 1917, while staying at a private hospital in London, Nichols was visited by Robert Graves. Nichols had become one of the most popular poets of the time, following publication of several of his verses. Graves enthused about Nichols and his poems to Siegfried Sassoon, but Sassoon and Nichols did not meet until November 1917 when they were both invited to dine by Robbie Ross at the Reform Club.

Sassoon admired Nichols' exuberant and confident nature and these two, with Robert Graves combined in a formidable literary triangle.

Robert Nichols, unlike Sassoon and Graves, felt no ambiguity with regards to his sexuality - he was a devout heterosexual. Graves' subsequent marriage to Nancy Nicholson and his dismissal of any previous homosexual tendencies led to Sassoon feeling somewhat isolated from his two friends as the years progressed.

Many letters exist between Sassoon and Nichols, written once Sassoon had returned to France, as Nichols became one of the few people in whom Sassoon felt he could confide his genuine feelings about the war.

Upon his return from his lecture tours in America at the end of the First World War, Nichols was engaged by Siegfried Sassoon (who had by now become Literary Editor of the *Daily Herald*) to write contributions for his newspaper column. The payment received for these writings aided Nichols' somewhat difficult financial situation.

In 1921, as well as becoming engaged to be married, Nichols left England for Japan where he took up the position of Professor of English at Tokyo University. He returned to London in the summer of 1922 to marry at St Martin's in Marylebone.

He remained in this teaching position until 1924, when he travelled to Hollywood. (His position in Tokyo was filled by Edmund Blunden). While in Hollywood, he was involved in one of the most exciting periods in the development of cinema and remained in America until the early 1930's writing theatre and screen-plays.

In 1933-4 he was living in Austria and Germany and witnessed the rise of Hitler but by the late 1930s he had settled in France. He left on the last ship carrying British refugees in June 1940.

During the Second World War, he worked as a writer and broadcaster until his death in Cambridge in the autumn of 1944.

Despite his forays into other forms of writing, his first love was always for poetry.

POETRY ANALYSIS

COMRADES: AN EPISODE

This poem tells the story of an officer, named Gates, who has been wounded and lies, dying, in No Man's Land. The poem opens with a description of how he came to be injured, and his certain knowledge, even while he is dressing his own wounds, that he will not survive.

The action then switches to the trench where his men, who have returned safely from the patrol, have become aware that their officer is missing and is lying injured on the barbed wire entanglements in front of the front line trenches.

One of the men, a corporal, believes he can go out and rescue Gates, but the approaching dawn, German guns firing and the arrival of another officer, prevent him. The corporal curses his bad luck, but, on hearing machine gun fire, the men believe that Gates must, by now, be dead anyway.

We now return to No Man's Land where Gates also witnesses the dawn. He begins to cry as he remembers home and understands that no-one will be able to come and rescue him. He notices the wind in the grass and a small aeroplane flying in the distance. Despite his attempts to heave himself up, he is too weak and finds it impossible to move. He resolves to die where he is, by himself. He seems more contented once he has reached this decision and begins to notice various things around him - the sun is shining and, somewhere in the distance, he can hear someone whistling a tune. He watches the day progress, knowing that, with it, his life is passing.

All of a sudden, Gates realises that he can hear the familiar voices of his own men in their trench, and mentally he pictures them. He finally resolves to get back to his men; his knowledge that he will die is certain, but he decides he would rather end his life in the company of these men whom he knows so well, than alone in No-Man's-Land.

He slowly drags his exhausted body back to the parapet of his own trench, but, upon reaching it, is too exhausted to lift himself over the top. Suddenly, he is spotted by a lookout, who shouts his name. Three of his men jump up to help him and two of them are shot and killed instantly. Gates is told the names of the dead men, Timmins and Jones, and is now distressed that his actions have cost their lives. His men reassure him that a doctor is on the way, but Gates dies before help can arrive.

This moving poem is written in the form of a story and, despite its rhyming couplets, reads almost like prose. The use of direct speech enhances this. Nichols describes the surroundings in language that is evocative and descriptive, helping the reader to realise that the dying man will no longer see all these beautiful, natural things which currently surround him. The whole poem has an atmosphere of quiet, assisted by his repetitive use of the word "whisper" - the men, the wind, even the shells are said to whisper. This calm, almost spiritual overtone helps to enhance the sense of death as a human tragedy.

The overriding theme of this poem is the love and comradeship between men and officers at the front. Nichols illustrates this as a reciprocal love. The corporal, for example, is happy - willing even - to risk his life to rescue Gates and is only prevented from doing so by another officer. It is interesting to note that the feeling of the corporal, when his attempt is halted, is shame: it would have been an honour to rescue Mr Gates - even at the risk to his own life.

This feeling was common where there was mutual respect and affection between men and officers and can be seen in many other works, including *Strange Meeting* by Susan Hill, where Parkin risks, and ultimately gives his life trying to help Hilliard.

The affection in which Gates holds his men can be seen in many ways, such as when he is able, upon hearing their voices, to picture a physical image of each one, listing particular features that spring to mind. His feelings are also made clear when he decides he must try to get back to them. He is not trying to get back to his trench in order to get treatment for his wounds: he knows that he will die. However, he has heard their voices in the distance and, thus reminded of them, he has come to realise how difficult it will be to die without seeing them one more time. We have already learnt that thinking about home and what he will miss there has reduced Gates to tears and yet in his final moments his only thoughts are not of home and family, but of his beloved men.

Nichols' poem is a celebration of male comradeship. He is not writing of the homo-erotic love that many poets hinted at, but of the powerful sense of friendship, togetherness and sharing which undoubtedly existed for many who served in the First World War. A good comparison with this could be *Journey's End* by R. C. Sherriff, where there is no mention, or even, it could be argued, hint of homosexuality, yet Osborne does not shy away from telling Hardy, right at the beginning of the play, that he loves Stanhope, thus setting the tone for much of what is to follow. All the men love and respect Stanhope - both as a man and an officer and he returns this affection. This form of love is born of shared hardships and experiences, together with a natural dependence on one's fellow soldier to do his job.

Comrades: An Episode is quite a difficult poem to categorise. It is not patriotic, nor does it glorify war, but, it is not anti-war either. It was written in 1915, before any of the other poets, such as Owen and Sassoon, had started writing their questioning and bitter poems. Yet, equally *Comrades* cannot be classed with Grenfell's *Into Battle* or Brooke's *1914* sonnets, both of which glorify war and death, albeit in different ways. Nichols treats death differently from many of his contemporaries. Brooke and Grenfell praised death as, most commonly, the safe sanctuary of those who have fought and died courageously for their country. Owen and Sassoon, ultimately portrayed death as a waste. For Nichols, particularly in *Comrades*, the image of death, while an inevitable part of war, is one of personal tragedy, grief and heartbreak.

This poem was, presumably, written either from observation or hearsay because Nichols, as an artillery officer, probably would not have experienced life in a front-line trench.

He wrote a similarly styled poem, which is more likely to have been based on his own experiences. This is called *Eve of Assault: Infantry Going Down to Trenches* and tells of a group of artillery soldiers who, waiting by their gun, are passed by a column of infantry, marching up towards the front. The two groups exchange words of encouragement with, in particular, the infantrymen urging the artillery to offer them protection in the forthcoming battle. The two groups part, but then, in the final two lines of the poem, we learn that the narrator (presumably, like Nichols, an officer) has been purely observing this, unable to join in the banter. Knowing that these men will die, he is too emotional even to speak, fearing that in doing so, his own heart will break. Again, death is displayed as inevitable and tragic - but never glorious.

Nichols speaks in many of his poems of love, grief and heroism and this, together with a lack of homo-erotic overtones, made his poetry very popular during the war years. He created an image of the war which was publicly acceptable.

WILFRED OWEN

BIOGRAPHY

Wilfred Edward Salter Owen was born on 18th March 1893 in Plas Wilmot near Oswestry in Shropshire. Until Wilfred was four the family lived in relative comfort in a house belonging to his grandfather, Edward Shaw - a former mayor of the city. Upon Shaw's death, it was discovered that he was virtually bankrupt and Wilfred and his family were forced to move to smaller lodgings in Birkenhead. Here they battled constant financial difficulties in attempting to maintain their previous lifestyle. This did not sit well with Wilfred's mother, Susan, who had an air of gentility and she determined that her beloved eldest son would, one day, restore the family fortune.

Wilfred had three siblings - a sister Mary and brothers Colin and Harold. He was closest in age to Harold, but as boys, these two were the least attached and it was not until later in life that they learned to appreciate each other's qualities.

Wilfred was educated at the Birkenhead Institute and under his mother's influence developed into an earnest and slightly arrogant young man. In 1907 the Owens moved again - this time to Shrewsbury as Wilfred's father, Tom, had been appointed Assistant Superintendent of the Joint Railways. Their living conditions improved, especially with the addition of open countryside which was now close at hand. Wilfred's seat of education became the Technical School in Shrewsbury where he studied hard. He enjoyed literature, having begun to write his own poems at about the age of ten and was then, as always, particularly influenced by the works of Keats.

In 1911 he sat the qualifying exam for London University and passed, but not with honours and, as his parents were unable to afford the fees, he required a scholarship which was out of the question. He took a position as lay assistant to the Vicar of Dunsden in Oxfordshire, in return for which he would receive tuition. This was not a happy time for Wilfred, who found his religious beliefs tested when confronted with the realities of the poor within the parish. The absence of his mother, who had been the greatest influence on his religious viewpoint, did not help matters. These doubts were fuelled by his growing interest in literature and, feeling that the two subjects were completely at odds, he decided to leave Dunsden in February 1913, returning to Shrewsbury. He then sat for a scholarship at Reading University, but failed and decided to put an end his ambition of a university education.

The financial position of the family meant that a career as a poet was impossible, so Wilfred decided to travel to France and work there as a teacher of English in the Berlitz School of Languages. This was no greater success than Dunsden and following an illness, he left in July 1914 and took up the position of private tutor to a wealthy family in the Pyrenees. In the autumn, however, he left this job and took up a similar one with another family which lasted until August 1915.

The outbreak of war initially had little effect on Owen, who continued with his life in France. In a letter to his mother from Bordeaux, dated 2nd December 1914, he speaks of his shame at not enlisting, but justifies this with the knowledge that he is perpetuating the English language: an ideal which he finds more important than any other.

By July 1915, he showed the first signs of a change of mind. In another letter to his mother, this time dated the 25th July 1915, he comments that, his inner happiness is now at stake. He says that he has decided to enlist as he can no longer continue to sit on the side-lines while others are fighting.

Owen returned to England in September 1915 and enlisted in the Artists' Rifles in October. Following months of training, he was commissioned into the Manchester Regiment in June 1916. Second Lieutenant Wilfred Owen arrived in France in late December 1916, right in the middle of the worst winter of the war. He was sent to Beaumont Hamel on the Somme as one of 527 reinforcements sent out following heavy losses in the Ancre Offensive.

On 13th March 1917, Owen fell into a cellar and received a concussion which hospitalised him for two weeks. On his return to his batallion at the beginning of April, he found himself involved in heavy fighting near St Quentin. He was blown off his feet by a shell in Savy Wood and spent several days in a shell-hole surrounded by the dismembered remains of a fellow officer. Although physically unhurt, when Owen's Battalion was relieved on 21st April, it was noticed that his behaviour had become abnormal - he was confused in his speech and appeared shaky. He was diagnosed as suffering from shell-shock and was sent to a Casualty Clearing Station. Eventually he was sent to Craiglockhart War Hospital in Edinburgh, where he would remain for four months.

While at Craiglockhart, Owen met Siegfried Sassoon, a fellow patient, and the two became friends. Sassoon's reputation as a poet and decorated war hero, had preceded him and the shy, stammering Owen was in awe, but plucked up his courage and introduced himself to the older man. After an initially awkward interview, Sassoon agreed to look at some of Owen's work. Whilst these early efforts were by no means brilliant, Sassoon perceived a natural talent hidden in Owens' poems. The more experienced poet encouraged and assisted his young protégé, even to the point where the manuscript of one of Owen's most famous poems, *Anthem for Doomed Youth*, contains nine amendments and several crossings-out in Sassoon's handwriting.

It was at this time, and also under the influence of Sassoon, that Owen wrote *Dulce et Decorum Est*, which was a response to the propagandist poems of Jessie Pope. Sassoon also took the opportunity to introduce Owen to Robert Graves, and through him Owen also met Robert Ross and H. G. Wells, among many others.

Owen was declared fit for light duties and left Craiglockhart for Scarborough. By the end of August he was back in France. Before leaving England he had told his brother, Harold, of his desire to return to the front, despite his, almost certain, knowledge that he would be killed. He had also, encouraged by Robert Ross and Osbert Sitwell, started planning a volume of poetry for publication.

In October 1918, he was awarded the Military Cross. The citation read:

"He personally manipulated a captured machine gun in an isolated position and inflicted considerable losses on the enemy. Throughout he behaved most gallantly."

On the morning of 4th November, while attempting to cross the Sambre-Oise Canal, Owen was shot and killed. One week later, the Armistice was signed, hostilities ceased and all over England, church bells rang out in celebration. Tom and Susan Owen were listening to these bells and looking forward to the safe return of their beloved eldest son when the telegram arrived announcing his death.

Wilfred Owen is buried in the tiny Commonwealth War Graves Commission cemetery at Ors.

Very few of Owen's poems were published during his lifetime and initially his work was not critically acclaimed. The first edition of his poems appeared in 1920, edited by Siegfried Sassoon and Edith Sitwell. It contained less than 25 of his poems.

It may have taken more than fifty years for Owen to gain the reputation he now holds, but he has become the most widely read and studied war poet.

POETRY ANALYSIS

SPRING OFFENSIVE

This was, in fact Owen's last poem. It was sent as an unfinished draft to Siegfried Sassoon and Owen questioned whether he should continue with it. He obviously decided to complete the poem and the final verse was written, very hurriedly, in pencil.

Owen had been involved in an attack the previous spring (1917) and his harrowing twelve days spent in the front line, forms the basis for Spring Offensive. In a letter written to his brother, Colin, in May 1917, Owen described the exhilarating yet horrifying sensation of going over-the-top and compared it to being in a dreamlike state in which everything moves in slow-motion.

The poem begins with the men at rest, some blissfully unaware of what awaits them, are able to sleep. It is late in the afternoon and the sky ahead of them is harsh and unforgiving. At the end of the first stanza, the men believe that they have reached a turning point. What lies ahead of them seems unknown - they cannot see what the future holds, possibly because they have no future. This signifies that those not asleep know and understand that a momentous task lies ahead of them, which may mark the end of their lives.

In the next stanza, Owen vividly describes a beautiful May scene, reminiscent of those spent in England and a reminder of all that is about to be lost. The summer (or sun) is like a drug, soothing their bodies. Remember that Owen had been in France during the previous, extremely harsh, winter: this would have made the warmth of the sun seem even more intense. The men, however, are morbidly aware of the grass over which they will attack. The harsh sky seems like a pane of glass - offering no freedom from the world in which they now find themselves.

The men are obviously kept waiting for some considerable while, giving them time to ponder their surroundings. They notice that, in walking through the fields of buttercups in the valley to the rear of them, some petals have become dislodged and attached to their boots. They have become allied with nature because it offers hope - nature survives despite the war which rages around it. The brambles on which they have, presumably, become caught, cling to them and clutch at their clothing. This is, in a way, reminiscent of the women left behind at home although it could also signify a sense that the earth will be sorry to lose these men and is trying to keep hold of them.

Then into this warm and comfortable picture intrudes the order to attack. There is no loud clamouring excitement, no flag-waving; just a short order and the men turn away from nature, and the sun. This signifies the men rejecting nature, turning their backs on the earth and, therefore, life. Yet, they seem to go happily, smiling into battle.

The fact that the men run together suggests jubilation and enthusiasm (as displayed by Owen in one of his letters home). The battle rages around them. Shell holes are, it would seem, created to hold the dead and dying - they are the perfect shape for such a task, like the communion cup, which holds the blood of Christ, while the shell holes hold the blood of the dead and dying men. The sensation of falling off a precipice is integrated here in his reference to sloping chasms and endless space. This also refers back to Owen's letter in which he described battle as being reminiscent of a dream-like state. The men don't see death approaching and their end is brutal and hellish. This is contrasted with the idea that these men are with God and that He will take care of them now.

The final stanza contrasts the eventual peace at the end of the battle with the heat and noise that formed its centre. Not everyone is dead - some survivors come back, but they are crawling - cowed and wrecked by their experiences. They don't speak of what they have witnessed or of friends lost. As in Sassoon's *Suicide in the Trenches*, they choose denial of what has gone before. The fact that this is stated as a question tells us that many were unsure why those that survived found it impossible to discuss their experiences.

EXPOSURE

The date for this poem is unknown, but it is thought that the events
it describes took place in Winter 1917, and that, in preparation for
the publication of his work, Owen made numerous changes to it
over the following year or so.

In a letter to his mother dated 4th February 1917, Owen describes
the extreme cold he had experienced in the trenches, vividly
describing the snow and icy wind. One of his men froze to death
and many ended up in hospital. They were heavily shelled, although
no-one was hurt as a result of this. He tells how the extreme cold
affected him physically, literally making his feet feel dead. He also
speaks of the unburied dead, pointing out how the sight of them,
sitting there, motionless day after day is enough to drain any
soldiers' spirits.

The title of the poem is the first point of interest. It naturally refers
to the exposure to the cold and the elements, but also to the fact
that these men are exposed in other ways - to enemy fire, to
constant potential danger, to boredom and ultimately death.

In the first stanza, Owen dramatically introduces the concept of
extreme cold, with his reference to the fact that the icy wind cuts
through the men, reminiscent of the bayonets used in battle. The
wind is therefore seen as having the same killing potential as a knife
or bayonet. The men are nervous because the night is so quiet and
they worry that this denotes an imminent attack. They are in a
salient, which is a place in the line which protrudes into enemy-held
territory and is, by definition, prone to heavy fighting. The ending of
this verse, and all the following ones, perpetuates the sense of
hopelessness and monotony.

The next two stanzas go on to further describe the awful
conditions: the elements are given human or natural characteristics,

so the wind is mad - like many of those who are experiencing these hardships. The barbed wire is like a bramble, and the dark clouds at dawn are an army. He continues this metaphor later in the poem where the wind is nonchalant and the snow touches their faces, like fingers. The coming of dawn does nothing to lift their spirits - there are no changes.

The description of the dawn as an army is possibly an allusion, not to a real army of men, but to the clouds which gather like a regiment preparing for battle, although in this case, they are heralding the arrival of more snow. This adds to the belief that the weather and conditions are as dangerous to the men as the enemy. However, this reference could also be interpreted as a hallucination of a forthcoming battle when you bear in mind that the German army wore grey uniforms. This battle obviously does not materialise, because, once again, nothing changes.

The fourth verse introduces the more conventional danger of bullets, but Owen informs us that they are less dangerous than the cold. At least a bullet would mean a quick death while the cold only provides a long, unrelenting suffering. There is so much snow that it has become impossible to see, hence the air is black - there is no hope and the blackness also represents the colour of death. The monotony continues with the snow being caught and drifted around by the wind, just as the men are drifting and helpless.

Although by the fifth stanza, it is daylight and the sun is shining, the men are still suffering - there is no respite from the cold - it is so hopeless that they begin to question whether death is actually upon them and the whole experience is one of dying. In these dreamy moments, their thoughts turn to the warmth - both literal and metaphoric - of home, as represented by the fires. But the doors are closed to these men and they come back to reality. These last two lines could imply that they know there is no future - no way back to a normal life and therefore to dream of home is futile. It could also be a reference to the frequently held concept that, due to the complacency and lack of understanding shown by those safe at home, these men belong more with their dead and dying comrades than with family and loved-ones.

In the seventh verse, Owen raises the idea that men *must* die; that this is the only means of securing the things which men hold dear. He tempers this, however, with the final line which tells us that even a love of God cannot survive these horrors.

The poem ends on the same hopeless note - the future only holds more of the same; they will die here in the frozen mud and become unrecognisable, even to their friends.

The use of sounds to describe the experience is vital in this poem. In the third stanza, we have similar sounding words which help to describe the monotony. In the fourth verse the ceaseless gathering snow is described using alliteration which only perpetuates the relentlessness of the snow, but also compares it with a flock of sheep, drifting aimlessly, so again we have a reference to a harsh nature and pointlessness.

In the final verse, the finishing lines perfectly demonstrate the finality of the piece, since it is through your eyes that you experience everything and they reveal all your emotions. The fact that all of the men's eyes are ice does not necessary mean that they are all dead, but could be interpreted that they have nothing left - no emotion left to feel and nothing more to give.

This poem could be compared with Isaac Rosenberg's *Dead Man's Dump*. Both of these poems seem to confuse the living and the dead, making much of the pointless waste and futile nature of the war. Owen and Rosenberg demonstrate their sense of hopelessness in the future: they can see little reason in anything. The descriptions of the men, and their surroundings in both of these poems are startlingly realistic, with nothing left to the reader's imagination, although Rosenberg's language is more harsh and gritty.

DISABLED

Although undated, this poem originates from some time before October 1917 as it was during that month that Siegfried Sassoon showed a draft of it to an enthusiastic Robert Graves, who greatly admired it.

It tells the story of a maimed soldier, who has lost both legs and one arm. He reminisces about his pre-war days and looks forward, grimly, to a bleak future. The theme of this poem is the waste and futility of war and the long term after-effects and suffering inflicted on the survivors. It is also an attack on the complacency of those at home.

The man is sitting in a wheelchair, bored and waiting for darkness to fall. The language used here illustrates the man's isolation, especially when compared to the warm and happy language used in the second verse. Even the voices of the children playing in the park are not seen as happy, and these are removed by their mothers, who take them home to bed; but he can neither join in nor follow.

He remembers how, before the war, this was the time of day when he used to go out and enjoy himself with the girls. We're told that he believes that the sacrifice of his limbs has been pointless. He realises that he won't be able to enjoy these pleasures any more - the girls all shun him, which reinforces his feelings of isolation.

He recalls how handsome he had been - an artist had wanted to paint him, but then he used to look young for his age. Now he seems old and wasted. He is colourless - lifeless - he lost his youth in the shell-holes of France. It is as though, with the loss of his limbs and the draining of his blood, his whole life has ebbed away.

We learn that before the war, he played football and would have been proud to receive an injury and be treated like a hero carried on the shoulders of his team-mates. This type of football injury contrasts with the spurting blood of his war-wound in the previous verse. However, just for the moment, he cannot even remember why he enlisted: was it vanity - because someone had said that a kilt would make him look even more handsome. This reference to kilts as well as some of the other language used, denote that this man would have served with a Scottish regiment, which is not that surprising since at the time this was written Owen would have been at Craiglockhart War Hospital near Edinburgh.

He questions whether he joined up to impress a girlfriend. He remembers how gladly and readily he had been accepted by the army, despite being underage. This fact, dropped unexpectedly, serves to enhance our pity for this man and tells us that he must still be very young. To him, enlisting and going out to France had been like a great adventure and he recalls the crowds cheering as he went away.

When he came back wounded, however, while there were more cheers, they were not celebratory, but the patriotic cheers of safe civilians. The happiness of the crowd cannot even be compared with their reaction to the scoring of a goal in a match of football. He feels that the people are ungrateful.

He knows he has a bleak future during which he will be completely dependant on the help of strangers. He realises, too, that he will be lonely as he is no longer attractive, or useful, to women. The final desperation of his question heightens the sense of this man's helplessness. He is unable to put himself to bed, let alone take a woman to bed with him. Many critics perceive a sexual theme within this poem. The man originally joined up to impress the women, but his youth and virility have been snatched from him. He is lonely and impotent, with no future or chance of happiness.

Owen makes use of colour and nature to demonstrate the difference between the past and the present. For instance, the present is a grey, cold colourless environment full of sadness and regret. He is in the winter of his life. The past is portrayed as colourful and gay, which makes that time seem more like summer - a time which this man never really had the opportunity to experience.

This disabled man is portrayed as lonely, abandoned by his friends, which is reminiscent of Margaret Postgate Cole's poem *The Veteran (May 1916)*, in which a blind soldier sits alone, offering advice to young soldiers. Although keen for the blind man's advice, the young, inexperienced men do not remain long, possibly because his plight reminds them of what might await them in France.

The soldiers in both poems appear to have grown old before their time: their experiences of the war having aged them. These two poems demonstrate the waste of youth - not through death, but through permanent disfigurement - which can never be recaptured.

Another poem worth contrasting with *Disabled* is *Who's For The Game?* by Jessie Pope, which compares the war to a game of football, urging young men to come and join in. This poem represents the loss of one's limbs as a worthy sacrifice, which contrasts well with the grim realities portrayed in *Disabled*.

DULCE ET DECORUM EST

This poem can be dated, fairly accurately, to October 1917 as Owen wrote of it, in a letter dated the 16th of that month. It was originally addressed directly to Jessie Pope who wrote patriotic verse at the time, but Owen was persuaded to change the subtitle to read "to a certain poetess", as to address Jessie Pope by name might have been considered inflammatory.

The theme of this poem is Owen's anger at the indifference of those at home who continued to propagate lies. You can see the influence of Siegfried Sassoon in this piece. The language is more direct and shocking than in much of Owen's other work and the poet has a particular grievance to air. The poem is narrated by a man who has witnessed this terrible ordeal.

The men, exhausted to a point near collapse, are going down the line and after a long march will reach a rest camp or billet where they will be able to sleep. They are so tired that personal discomfort no longer bothers them - even the dropping of shells fails to rouse them from their oblivion as they march, and they have gone beyond tiredness into an almost dreamlike state. It could be argued that these men have become ghost-like during their stay at the front, hence the flares which they are leaving behind haunt them as they go.

But then, unexpectedly, they are awoken from their metaphorical slumber by an alarm - a warning of gas. They panic and fumble with their gas-masks, denoting the rush of adrenaline this attack has caused. One man, however, fails to fit his mask in time and the narrator describes the victim stumbling around in a blind panic, as though he were on fire - unsure which way to turn, yet knowing that he will die.

Through the visor of his own gas helmet, he witnesses the man appearing to drown. This is an apt description as victims of mustard gas choked to death on their own blood.

This vision is something which haunts the narrator - he wonders if he could have done anything to help. The victim plunging at him suggests he was desperately seeking help which the narrator was unable to give. The language and repetition used here reinforces the sense of doom and finality which await the victim.

The poem now changes tone and pace. Owen addresses the people at home and suggests to them that if, in their worst nightmares, they could re-live this experience, they would not keep repeating that it is good and sweet to die for your country. He is saying that no-one who has witnessed these horrors could ever encourage anyone to take part in such a war.

The language of the final verse is necessarily shocking and harsh. They fling the man into a wagon, because they know there is no point in being gentle - he will soon be dead anyway. The description of his face and eyes gives him a ghost-like quality. This verse is intended to demonstrate the realism of a violent, unnecessary death, hence it builds to a crescendo of anger, before a final earnest plea to stop the lies.

This sense of anger at those who were deemed to be sitting, safely and complacently at home, is quite common in First World War poetry, and literature. Siegfried Sassoon's poems are frequently and bitterly directed at those who he felt had little or no understanding of the suffering of the troops. This theme is also shown in the novel *Birdsong* by Sebastian Faulks. One of the officers, Michael Weir, having been home on leave, becomes extremely angry about the attitude of civilians, who believe that they do understand the realities of the war, simply because they have read about it in the newspapers.

ANTHEM FOR DOOMED YOUTH

This sonnet was completed on the 25th September 1917 and went through many drafts before reaching this stage, with the final manuscript bearing several alterations made by Siegfried Sassoon. This is probably Owen's best-known and most-studied poem.

The poem begins by comparing the deaths of soldiers with the death of cattle in a slaughterhouse. Neither receives a proper Christian funeral. This comparison also suggests that Owen believes the men are treated like cattle in life as well as death.

Through the use of aural imagery, Owen states that the only ones to mourn the men on the battlefield are the guns and shells which have preyed upon and now killed them. One could argue that the guns are monstrously angry and the shells wail dementedly because, once the men are dead, they will have no-one left to kill. The customary Christian burial trappings of prayers, bells and choirs are dismissed as mockeries and replaced with the weapons which have destroyed them. The final line of the first stanza, however brings the reader home to the playing of The Last Post, and the sadness of those left grieving at home.

It is clear that these men will not receive a funeral in the conventional sense. If they are lucky enough to be buried, it will probably be a quick ceremony with no mourners. Owen's use of visual imagery in the second verse contrasts it further with the first; now we are concerned with those left behind. He talks of tearful boys, whose shiny eyes will replace the candles as they say goodbye. This could be a reference to the fact that many of the men with whom the dead have served are little more than boys themselves, and could, therefore, be seen as representative of alter-boys, or choir-boys at a conventional funeral. They cannot hold candles at the front, but the shining tears in their eyes will reflect their true feelings.

There will be no traditional pall (a cover for a coffin), so the only thing these men can take with them to the grave, is their memories of young girls and lost love. There will be no flowers laid for these dead, instead they will be remembered in the minds of those they have left behind. The final line is a reference to the tradition of closing the blinds or curtains of a house, for a period of time, after the death of a household member. In this instance, Owen could be saying that, at every dusk, these men will be remembered - in other words the mourning will go on forever.

This poem shows Owen's realisation that the war will affect everyone. Although this is a sad, reflective poem, there is also a hint of bitterness and anger in that Owen seems to feel that the men are being treated and slaughtered like cattle. He appears to be alluding to the fact that all trappings of civilisation have been lost to these men, and they are not even allowed the respect normally given to the dead.

The allusion to dusk in the final line could be a reference to Laurence Binyon's *For the Fallen* which Owen had read in 1915. The fourth verse of this poem is quoted every year at Remembrance Day services around the world.

In *Anthem for Doomed Youth* Owen is, in his own way, urging our respect and remembrance for the dead.

THE PARABLE OF THE OLD MAN AND THE YOUNG

In order to understand this poem it is essential to first read Genesis, Chapter 22, verses 1-19, which contains the story of Abraham and Isaac. This is the story of how God speaks to Abraham and issues him with a test of his faith. Abraham receives instructions that he must take his beloved only son Isaac to the land of Moriah, where he must sacrifice him. Abraham follows God's instructions and, while he and Isaac are walking to the place designated for the offering, Isaac asks his father where the lamb is, which they are here to sacrifice. Abraham lies to his son, and says that God will provide a lamb for the offering. Abraham builds the alter, binds his son and takes out the knife with which he intends to kill him. Then suddenly an Angel of the Lord calls to him and says that he should not harm the boy as, by merely offering him for sacrifice, he has proved his faith in God. Abraham notices a ram which is caught by his horns in a thicket and offers that as a sacrifice instead of Isaac. Again the Angel of the Lord speaks to Abraham, telling him that, because of his loyalty, he and his offspring will be blessed, all-conquering and as numerous and the stars in the sky.

Owen's poem follows this story, almost word-for-word, with only a few, notable, exceptions. For example, in the biblical version, no mention is made of the implements used by Abraham to bind his son, but Owen refers to these as straps and belts, which could be a reference to parts of a soldiers uniform. This may indicate that Owen perceives these as a symbol of entrapment, binding the men to their fate and preparing them for their sacrifice. The original story depicts Abraham as building an alter upon which to sacrifice his son, while Owen has him build trenches and parapets. This demonstrates Owen's perception that the men in the trenches were being slaughtered, like sacrificial offerings. Owen refers to the ram which is caught in the thicket as the Ram of Pride which again differs from the Bible's version where there is no such reference. Here Owen appears to be saying that the only way to avoid making the sacrifice is the surrender one's pride instead. Finally, and most importantly, Owen's old man chooses to slay his son, and with him, half of the men of Europe, individually. There are many implications to this ending: for example, Owen's old man will not have numerous offspring, because in killing a generation of men, the line will end; Owen seems to believe that the old are sacrificing the young, merely to save their own pride.

Other interesting points to note in this poem include the fact that in the original story, Abraham lies to Isaac, telling him that God will provide a sacrificial lamb, whereas in Owen's poem, Abraham makes no response to this question at all. This suggests that Owen believes there is no explanation for the slaughter. It is, in fact, quite curious that, in Owen's poem, Abraham does *not* lie, especially as this is an accusation which Owen had levelled at various sectors of society in other poems.

Another noteworthy point is that, in Owen's poem, the old man slays the young men individually. This makes their deaths more personal than mass slaughter, and gives their deaths an air of murder being committed by the old. Also, Owen says that it is the sons of Europe who are being slaughtered: not only Britain or the Allied nations, but the whole continent is suffering.

The messages in this poem are numerous: Owen holds the old responsible for the deaths of the young, because the old would rather thoughtlessly sacrifice a generation of young men, than relinquish their nationalistic pride. He also appears to imply that the soldiers are bound to their fate, as though physically tied. In giving the war a religious connection, it could be argued that he, in some way, blames God for the war and the deaths of so many.

The use of religious imagery in First World War literature is not unusual. In 1916 Robert Graves wrote *Goliath and David*, which re-tells the story of David and Goliath from the book of Samuel (chapter 17, verses 1-58). Graves turns this parable on its head, however, as his David - here representing Lieutenant David Thomas - is defeated by Goliath who represents the Germans. (David Thomas was a handsome young lieutenant who was shot in the throat and killed on 18th March 1916. Thomas' death was the inspiration behind Graves' poem and also inspired his fellow Royal Welch Fusilier, Siegfried Sassoon to write his beautiful poem *The Last Meeting*). In portraying Goliath as the conqueror Graves paints a fairly hopeless and depressing picture. Although David continually swings his pebbles at the Giant, it is to no avail, as Goliath overpowers him. In other words, the innocence and beauty of youth have no hope of survival when pitched against the brutish reality of battle.

Another poem with definite religious overtones is *Christ and the Soldier* by Siegfried Sassoon. This poem does not depict a specific biblical story, but tells of a soldier who comes across a roadside sculpture, depicting the Crucifixion. The soldier enters into an imagined conversation with Christ in which he tries to make sense of the horrors of the war. Christ cannot offer any explanation, other than to fall back on tried and tested Christian values and precepts. Eventually, the soldier asks why he was even born at all and to this question he receives no answer, except the continuous noise of battle. Sassoon in this poem is questioning the value of religion and the ability of the clergy to cope with the events unfolding before them.

All three poets, despite having religious upbringings, seem to have become doubtful as to their faith and its place in their world. Owen's poem, in sticking very closely to the original text from the bible, is probably the most shocking, especially as he manages to conceal his amendment to the end of the story until the last two lines of the poem. Graves does not achieve the same effect because, even in the title, he has revealed his intentions by placing Goliath's name before David's. By the end of the second verse the reader is in no doubt of the outcome.

The concept of questioning religious beliefs is also portrayed in *Birdsong* by Sebastian Faulks in which one of the main characters, Jack Firebrace, finds himself unable to understand how a wise and forgiving God in whom he has always believed, could allow such atrocities to take place. The padre, Horrocks, also throws away his silver cross in disgust after witnessing the massacre on the battlefields of the Somme.

In *The Parable of the Old Man and the Young*, Owen is using religion against those he considers to be responsible for the carnage - namely the old. The older generation, generally speaking, placed far more importance upon religion than the young and as such, Owen is really using one of their own weapons against them by questioning their commitment to anything other than their own self-preservation.

THE SEND-OFF

This poem ostensibly gives the soldier's view of a farewell at a railway station. The scene is set at dusk and the train is full of young men going out to the front. The fact that the men have been singing while they marched down to the station is not unusual - marching songs were sung throughout the war and helped to revive flagging spirits. Once aboard the train, their faces are described as grim and yet happy - a contradiction in terms. The men have come from a nearby camp, which implies that they have been in training, rather than on leave and suggests that they may be new recruits. Thus, their expressions are born of inexperience - they are worried and nervous, but maintain a brave countenance.

The flowers which they wear on their tunics resemble those of a funeral, which reminds us that these men are as good as dead. The porters who see them leave seem drab by comparison with the soldiers - this is a scene they often witness and to which they have grown accustomed. The tramp is sorry to see the men go, but this sorrow is not necessarily for them: he will miss their presence at the camp - presumably they have been generous towards him.

Then, as though complicit in some sort of conspiracy, the signals seem to nod - a sign of approval - and the lamp winks to demonstrate the imminent departure of the train. The description of these movements signifies a sort of underhand, silent agreement which is perpetuated in the beginning of the next verse, where the men are seen to leave in secret, as though there is some shame or embarrassment attached to their departure. Although they are closely observed as they leave, these men are not related to anyone at the station and, therefore their destination, and their fate, will remain unknown. No-one will ever know what happens to them or how they will feel once they reach the front and discover the horror of the war. Owen wonders how, having made this discovery, the men will feel about the women who sent them away with flowers - will they ever understand whether the flowers were given in happiness or regret, or as a precursor to their deaths.

Finally, he wonders whether these men will ever come back again and whether their return will be thought of in terms of a victory. He concludes that there will not be enough of them to make their homecoming worthy of celebration. Instead, when they do come back home, he believes that their experiences will have changed them forever, making their once-familiar surroundings seem strange. In this final verse, there is, again, an air of conspiracy and shame: once more the men must be silent, although perhaps this time their silence denotes the fact that they will no longer be able to share their thoughts and feelings because the war will have changed their outlook so much.

This poem is thought to have been written in 1918 and Owen altered the manuscript many times before its completion. Some critics consider this to be one of Owen's finest poems. His message here is a criticism of those safely left behind on the home front. He demonstrates throughout that there is an air of silent collusion against the soldiers: for example, the signal and lamp at the station are given conspiratorial human traits of nodding and winking. These pieces of equipment are obviously incapable of feeling for the men, but this enforces the idea that everything around the soldiers is conspiring against them.

The people at the station are portrayed similarly: they do not care about these particular men. For the porters, the tramp and the women, there will be other trains carrying different men on another day. The men are seen to be anonymous and are given no names. In fact, it seems that there is nobody familiar to see them off, which makes the poem more impersonal and links back to the uncaring attitude of those at home.

Owen makes great use of contradictions in this poem: for example, the men are described as grim, yet happy; the signal is unmoved (or unsympathetic) and yet it nods; the flowers can been seen as a farewell gift or a funeral wreath. This intentional ambiguity enhances the air of conspiracy and the darkness of the poem, which surfaces in particular towards the end. Here, although Owen acknowledges there may be survivors, he does not anticipate a great celebration upon their return. Instead, he believes that, once the war is over, people will just want to forget about it and that through either choice or necessity, the survivors will have to remain silent. However, he acknowledges that the men themselves will have changed - their surroundings will no longer be familiar to them. This may imply that the men will be away for a long time and will forget much of what they have left behind, or that their experiences will change them so much that nothing will ever be the same again.

At no time in this poem do the soldiers appear to be appreciated. They are going to a mysterious and dangerous future and yet their departure goes almost unnoticed. The only person who regrets them leaving is the tramp, but this is only for selfish reasons and not because he really cares about them.

Many poems of the First World War directed criticism against the complacency of those at home. Quite often this was done with the use of bitter satire, particularly by Siegfried Sassoon. In The Send-Off, however, Owen refrains from the use of this technique. He does not use harsh language or direct criticism - everything is implied and in all probability that is what makes the poem so powerful and thought-provoking.

ISAAC ROSENBERG

BIOGRAPHY

Dovber Rosenberg left his native Lithuania for Britain in 1887, settling initially in Leeds and then moving to Bristol. Upon arrival he had changed his christian name to Barnet, but throughout his life, found it difficult to gain employment. Eventually he found work as a pedlar and was joined by his wife Hacha (who became known as Anne), and their daughter Minnie, who was nine years older than her brother, Isaac who was born on 25th November 1890. By this time, Barnet had found employment as a drapery dealer, but life was still hard for the family. Young Isaac was instantly adored by his astute and robust mother, whose naturally protective nature may have been intensified by the fact that Isaac's twin brother had died at birth, and that Isaac, even as a child, was never physically strong. Barnet and Anne lived an impoverished life and had a hostile relationship, yet by 1899, they had had another four children: Annie, Rachel, David and Elkan.

In 1897, they moved to Stepney in the East End of London, where they joined a close Jewish community and were able to feel more settled. Although they were now in happier surroundings, poverty continued to blight the Rosenbergs and Anne took on odd jobs of mending, sewing and laundry to supplement Barnet's income. These were difficult times for young Isaac, whose artistic nature soon became apparent. His parents, however, accepted this side of their son's personality, and did everything in their power to assist him. Isaac initially attended St Georges in the East Board School, before moving to the Baker Street Board School in 1899. Here his obvious talents for art were recognised and encouraged and he began attending the Stepney Green Art School for additional art lessons. At this stage he also began to take an interest in poetry, developing a particular taste for Keats and Byron.

Aged just fourteen, Isaac left school in 1904 and, keen to assist him in his artistic career, his parents found him a position as an apprentice engraver at a company called Carl Hentschel's in Fleet Street in London. Mr and Mrs Rosenberg undoubtedly meant well, but this was by no means the profession to which Isaac aspired, and he soon became demoralised. He appreciated, however, that his family needed his financial contribution, so he remained in this employment for many years.

In the meantime, craving literary and artistic stimulation, he joined The Whitechapel Group, which was an assembly of aspiring writers. Although this assuaged his desire to write, he still felt like an outsider and found it difficult to make friends. In order to advance his artistic skills, Isaac enrolled in classes at the Birkbeck Institute. Here, surrounded by fellow artists, who included, amongst others, Paul Nash, Isaac's work impressed his tutor. He concentrated mainly on life drawings and won many prizes. In 1911, Rosenberg finally left Hentschel's, intending to pursue his career as an artist. His initial happiness at this new-found freedom soon turned to despair when he discovered that ambition and talent were insufficient qualities to guarantee commissions. While sketching at the National Gallery, he met Mrs Herbert Cohen, who introduced him to Mrs Delissa Joseph and Mrs Henrietta Lowy. These wealthy Jewish benefactors sponsored Isaac and paid his tuition fees at the Slade School of Art, which he first attended in October 1911.

Although Isaac enjoyed his studies and made excellent progress, he found it difficult to settle. The Slade contained a wide variety of students from different backgrounds, but Isaac felt that his lack of breeding and ready income were putting him at a disadvantage to his fellow students.

Rosenberg also found time to write poetry and in 1912 he summoned the courage to send some manuscripts to Laurence Binyon. Binyon was already an established poet and author, and is most famous for writing the often quoted poem *For the Fallen*, the fourth verse of which is recited every year at countless Remembrance Day Services. Rosenberg received great encouragement from Binyon and continued enthusiastically with his writing.

In November 1913, Rosenberg was introduced to Edward Marsh, who featured in the lives of many First World War poets. A senior civil servant of independent means, Marsh would later become private secretary to Winston Churchill. He edited and published *Georgian Poetry*, a series of influential anthologies, and encouraged many aspiring poets, including Wilfred Wilson Gibson, Rupert Brooke and Siegfried Sassoon, among many others. Rosenberg and Marsh corresponded regularly throughout the remainder of Rosenberg's life.

Leaving The Slade in March 1914, Rosenberg faced two immediate problems: his formal training had done nothing to improve his financial predicament; and his health had taken a turn for the worse. In order to ease both of these problems, he decided to leave Britain and in June, he set sail for South Africa to stay with his sister Minnie, who had recently married and moved there.

His time in South Africa proved productive - he found the atmosphere and the people stimulated his writing; and the light gave his paintings a new perspective. When war was declared in August, Rosenberg found no urgent necessity to return home and delayed doing so until May 1915. Upon his return he published a pamphlet entitled Youth, and received a few commissions for paintings, but as the war dragged on, the public became less interested in the art and poetry of those who remained at home.

By October 1915, Rosenberg's financial situation had become desperate, so he decided to enlist, although he kept this a secret from his family. One of his reasons for enlisting was that half of his pay would be sent home to his mother and although his family needed this additional income, she would have been devastated to know that her son had enlisted to benefit the family finances. Having an aversion to killing, Rosenberg tried to enlist with the Royal Army Medical Corps, but his physique was too poor, so he was sent to join a Regiment of "Bantams", formed specifically for men under 5' 3" tall. He went to the 12th Suffolk Regiment, until January 1916 when he was transferred to the 12th South Lancs. From here, he was sent to complete his training with the 11th Battalion, Kings Own Royal Lancasters.

Rosenberg remained a Private throughout his army career, but found it difficult to socialise with his fellow soldiers: his intellect was, generally speaking, far superior and his artistic nature grated with the other men. He was over-sensitive, clumsy and absent-minded, which gave rise to his captain dubbing him as "completely hopeless" as a soldier. Despite this, he was sent out to France in June 1916 and went into the trenches near Béthune with the 40th Division. He did not settle well into the harsh realities of trench life, finding the lice, rats and filth intolerable.

Unlike many other "soldier-poets", who were officers, Rosenberg, as a private, lacked any form of conducive surroundings or company. Even acquiring writing paper was difficult and occasionally he would resort to using lavatory paper for this purpose. These hardships did not prevent him from writing, however, and that autumn he wrote, arguably, his most famous poem *Break of Day in the Trenches*.

As the cold, damp winter approached, Rosenberg's lung problems were exacerbated. His family pleaded with Edward Marsh to use his influence and get Rosenberg removed from the trenches. Marsh managed to arrange for a medical examination, but the outcome was that the young poet was declared fit for trench work. In many ways he was unsuited to a soldier's life, particularly due to his absent-mindedness which often resulted in him being punished for some misdemeanour.

In March 1917, Rosenberg was afforded a change of scene when his company was removed from the trenches and sent behind the lines to help with the building and repair of roads and railways. After an uneventful summer, he was finally granted some home leave. He naturally enjoyed seeing his mother again, but like many soldiers, he found it difficult to adjust to life on the home front.

Back in France, the Bantams, as a unit, were virtually decimated in Bourlon Wood that Autumn, but Rosenberg escaped this slaughter, having been hospitalised at the beginning of October, suffering from influenza. The more comfortable surroundings of the hospital made it easier for him to write more freely. Upon his release from hospital in December, he voiced his wish to be transferred to the Jewish Battalion in Mesopotamia. He believed that the climate there would better suit his health, and he also wished to escape from any anti-semitic elements within the army, both real and perceived. Despite his sister's pleas to Edward Marsh, nothing became of this.

March 21st 1918 saw the beginning of the German Spring Offensive and by this time Rosenberg was back in the reserve line trenches. The initial German advance moved so rapidly, however, that Rosenberg soon found himself in the front line.

On the night of March 31st, he went out on a routine patrol and was killed in the early hours of April 1st. The fact that someone so young and obviously talented should die on April Fools' Day, many say, demonstrates the unnecessary and hopeless waste that the First World War had become.

Initially, he was buried on the battlefield with nine other men and a list was made of those interred, but the grave was left unmarked. Much later, in 1926, this grave was discovered and the ten bodies were removed to Bailleul Road East Cemetery. Although the men were unable to be individually identified, the Commonwealth War Graves Commission decided that each man should have his own headstone. The following year, Rosenberg's family asked the Commission, and was given leave, to add the words "Artist and Poet" to his headstone.

It is now a widely held opinion that his artistic abilities gave Rosenberg's poetry a unique quality, as he looked at his surroundings through the more detached eyes of an artist, rather than a soldier or poet. This temperament also worked against him and his mental state was greatly affected by his wartime experiences, causing him to assert in his last letter (to Edward Marsh), that even his ability to write poetry had become diminished. Whether or not this is the case will, of course, never be known: that he wrote some of the most thought provoking and evocative poetry of his time, is beyond doubt.

POETRY ANALYSIS

BREAK OF DAY IN THE TRENCHES

The title of this poem automatically inspires hope in the reader: the break of day representing a new beginning and new hope. Even in the trenches, one is inclined to believe, it might have been possible to wake up feeling thus, even if only because, momentarily, one had forgotten the war.

The first line, however, immediately lowers the spirits. Light is beginning to break through as dawn approaches, but this event is not heralded with any degree of optimism. The word 'crumbling' used here has more than one connotation: it could suggest the literal crumbling of the parapet, which would be the soldier's view as he looked towards the dawn; alternatively it could be used to demonstrate the disintegration of the mens' lives and their world. One could also argue that 'crumbling', being quite a gloomy word, suggests that the coming dawn is not a cheerful event, but merely marks the beginning of another monotonous day; that the days merge together - no one being better or more worthwhile than the previous.

This sense of timelessness continues into the next line; the language here serving to reiterate the feelings of boredom and monotony. Giving the word 'Time' a capital letter brings to mind Old Father Time and evokes an image of an old man, representing the passing years. The mention of a druid represents an ancient religious group renowned for, amongst other things, performing human sacrifices, usually at dawn. This could be interpreted as a suggestion that the soldiers are themselves being sacrificed, and will, therefore, not experience the full passage of time, as their lives will have been wasted. It should also be remembered that dawn was a frequently chosen time of day for launching attacks, on the basis of taking advantage of half-light, and catching the enemy unawares before he had fully woken up. For this reason, companies in the front line trenches would "stand-to" at dawn, before breakfast, and await any potential enemy attacks. This probably enhanced the association between sacrifice and that particular time of day.

In the third line, the poet seems to imply that everything around him is dead, except the live thing which has just leaped over his hand. Then, however, he informs us that this 'live thing' is a rat. Traditionally associated with death and disease, this rat is mocking and triumphant as though it believes that it has conquered the men.

Suddenly, in line five, an element of natural beauty is introduced, contrasting greatly with the perceived ugliness of the rat, and the darkness and monotony of the first two lines. However, this beauty is tempered by the reminder that the poppy has come from the parapet, which we already associate with crumbling disintegration. Without in the least admiring its beauty, he sticks the poppy behind his ear, just like a pencil or a cigarette. This demonstrates that the poppy has little significance, compared to the rat.

The poet seems to find the rat oddly amusing, but suggests that his fellow soldiers would shoot the vermin if they understood, as he in fact does, that the rat does not care where he gets his food from; he is not their loyal companion: he is selfish and concerned only for his own survival. The description of the rat's nature as 'cosmopolitan' demonstrates this, as he believes that the whole world is his to enjoy, the war being, to him, just an excellent means of acquiring food. Despite the rat's sub-human nature, the way he is described in this poem also allows him an almost human quality. It could be interpreted that Rosenberg's humanising of the rat demonstrates that to him, the men are like rats, concerned only with their own survival and killing

He tells us that the rat will, of course, cross from one trench to another, with no perception of 'enemy' or 'friend', but purely to feast on whatever is most readily available. The rat can cross No Man's Land without fear - unlike the men and, therefore, this journey is perceived as something pleasant, whereas it is something which the men fear. Again, the rat is triumphant - this ability to cross over No Man's Land unimpeded places the rat above the men. Although it is not unheard of, it is fairly unusual to refer to No Man's Land as 'green'. Possibly this colour is being used ironically, or to represent that things outside the trench are living normally, like the poppy. It also provides an excellent internal rhyme with the words before and after. The fact that this area is described as sleeping is also interesting. There are, we learn later, dead bodies lying in No Man's Land, so perhaps Rosenberg, like many other poets, perceives the dead as merely sleeping. Or possibly, he is implying that, at least while no battle rages, the land itself may sleep.

The poet imagines the wry, almost gloating, smile of the rat as he scuttles past dead bodies en route, yet he describes these bodies not in terms of death or decay, but using strong, vivid language reminding us of the mens' best physical qualities when they were alive. These dead men, he asserts, have not been so fortunate as the rat. It is interesting to note that he doesn't compare the dead men's misfortune with himself but with the rat. This makes the reader question whether he feels that the rat is better off than all of them - both the living and the dead; or whether he feels that he may as well be dead himself.

Now the tone and language change and the dead men are no longer allowed the physical qualities he previously gave them. He claims that they have been murdered on a whim. The fact that he describes the dead as being bound to their murderers implies that the guilty party is the person - or institution - paying them. In this case that would either be the army or the politicians. The image of death he creates here is more gritty and realistic. Describing their resting place as the very centre of the earth suggests that the land itself has been wounded or cut open, an image which is reiterated in the description of the ravaged fields in which they now lie.

He then enquires, presumably of the rat, whether he can perceive fear in the eyes of the dead. It is worth noting that he says 'our eyes', not '*their* eyes' which, again, suggests that he associates himself more with the dead than the living. The shells and guns are described as 'shrieking' while the sky is a 'still' heaven. Perhaps he is ironically suggesting that the earth now is more like Hell than Heaven. It seems that he is now mocking the rat, challenging it to find a symptom of fear in the mens' eyes - where he knows that there will be no demonstration of feeling whatsoever. The fact that these are 'our' eyes, however, suggests that he is also beyond fear.

Suddenly we are returned to the image of the poppy, but again, not to admire its beauty. Having their roots in the veins of the men could be a comparison with the colour of the flower and blood; or he could be implying that as the mens' bodies rot into the soil, the poppies 'feed' on them - just like the rat. Again, he returns to an image of death: the poppies keep dying - just like the men, in a seemingly endless cycle.

The poet believes, quite falsely of course, that the poppy behind his ear is safe. He forgets that in picking the flower, he has killed it. This affords the poppy the same arbitrary sense of impending death as the men. Also the flower is now bound to its murderer as were the men. Being behind the poet's ear is by no means safe, but does imply that their deaths, or lives, are linked. It is as though he feels the poppy gives him a sense of security. The poppy, he says, is white with dust, which could be a reference to the words used in a funeral service: 'ashes to ashes, dust to dust'. This might confirm that he knows that the flower and (by connection) the poet himself, are already dead - or as good as.

This is a bleak poem, devoid of hope for the future. The poet does not mention any other people, except the dead; in fact the only other living thing is the rat. The poppy, once picked, is dead. It is as though, thus surrounded by death, Rosenberg feels drawn towards that state himself. Both the rat and the poppies are deemed to be feeding off the dead men, thus giving them a element of triumph and superiority.

There is a feeling of monotony in this poem: time does not appear to move on; there is no progress, other than that of the rat. This could be said to be reminiscent of Wilfred Owen's *Exposure*, which relates the tedious and pointless waste that epitomises the lives of the soldiers; as though those who are still alive should be *unfavourably* compared with the dead. Another poem which warrants some comparison with *Break of Day in the Trenches* is Siegfried Sassoon's *Prelude: The Troops*. The vocabulary and language used in these two poems is quite similar. For example, both mention the dawn as a dreary, gloomy time of day: for Rosenberg it crumbles, while for Sassoon it is dull and grey - neither of these descriptions give the reader any feeling of the usual optimism associated with daybreak. Both poets suggest that the men are being murdered - this is strong language which leaves no doubt as to an author's viewpoint, or the feeling that a great proportion of blame should be attached to those deemed responsible. In both poems, there is a reference to green grass, but in neither case is this used to represent hope or life, but is more a reminder that such thoughts and aspirations have been abandoned. These two poems also share an allusion to dust: Rosenberg appears to hint at a funeral service, while Sassoon refers to entire armies of men who have become dust.

Rosenberg's poem was written in the autumn of 1916, while Sassoon's appears to have been produced towards the end of 1917, and like much of his work, makes his anti-war, anti-establishment viewpoint very clear. Both poems share a similar message: that the war is a gargantuan waste and completely futile; both point a finger of blame; and both, without upholding the war in any virtuous manner, praise and pity its victims.

Unlike Sassoons' or indeed Owens' poems, however, there is no bitterness or anger in *Break of Day in the Trenches*. It is infinitely more matter-of-fact - as though Rosenberg feels that he is merely stating the obvious

RETURNING, WE HEAR THE LARKS

This poem opens with the men marching back from the front to a rest-camp. Rosenberg describes the night as sombre or gloomy and points out that the soldiers fear the night because it heralds untold dangers. These men are obviously exhausted as they drag their tired bodies back towards the camp, and the comparative safety it holds. Here they will be able to sleep, even if only for a short time, away from the danger and discomfort of the front line. The road down which they march is described as blasted by poison, which denotes that it has obviously been shelled, either literally by poison gas shells, or that Rosenberg perceives all shells as deadly - like poison.

Then the tone changes as the poet hears birdsong. The repetition, three times, of the word 'joy' symbolises the unusual nature of this emotion for these men, which is reiterated by the fact that this is deemed by the poet as being strange. The dark night no longer seems fearsome, but is now filled with beautiful birdsong. An image is being created of these battle-weary men, who have tramped, exhausted from the front line, and are completely overwhelmed by the unseen beauty they have discovered. They turn their faces towards the blank sky and the birdsong falls like a gentle shower of rain, soaking their senses with its invisible harmony.

A jolt back to reality follows, as the poet states the bare fact that, just as birdsong appears to be 'raining' from the sky, so could a shell - unforeseen until it is too late. This takes the reader back to the realism of the poet's situation, in that death, during the First World War, was as everyday and commonplace as birdsong in peacetime.

Then comes partial reassurance as we learn that the only thing which *has* dropped from the sky is the birdsong. However, he says, this is only the equivalent to the shattering of a dream, because the danger which will destroy them, and their dreams themselves, are both invisible, and will arrive unannounced, one bringing beauty and peace, the other destruction. He compares this sense of unseen, yet impending doom with that of a blind man, who waits on the sand while the tide comes in, unable to move.

At the end of the poem, it is as though the poet is saying that behind every thing of beauty lurks danger and death. He appears here to be criticising women as he says that in their kisses they have a hidden danger. This could be an allusion to the women who appeared to gladly send their men to war with a kiss, or goaded them into joining up, little dreaming that such action would bring death and destruction. He is not comparing a woman's beauty very favourably with the lark's birdsong, but perhaps it is the uncomplicated nature of the song which endears it to the poet, rather than the physical attraction, and implied danger, of a beautiful woman.

Nature, in the form of birds, animals, flowers etc., is often used in First World War poetry as a means of forming a contrast between the beauty and peace of home, with the harsh realities of war. Examples of this can be seen in the works of many poets, for instance: Rupert Brooke, Edward Thomas and Laurence Binyon among countless others. The contrast here, however, is that many of these poets use these images of 'home' to symbolise a nationalist pride, which attempts to justify, at least to some extent, the fighting (and, in some cases, to positively encourage it). Rosenberg, on the other hand, as an experienced and war-weary private soldier, uses such images to portray the sense, demonstrated in this poem, that destruction lurks everywhere - even in nature at its most beautiful. This poem creates the impression that he feels surrounded, and overwhelmed, by death.

DEAD MAN'S DUMP

This poem begins with a description of artillery being drawn up a track towards the front. It is described as being rusty which denotes its age and the amount of use it has seen. The guns are given an air of authority with the use of the word 'sceptre', implying power; and also of sacrifice from the symbolism of the thorny crown, reminiscent of that worn by Christ at the Crucifixion. The guns serve a useful purpose, however: they halt the enemy who are described as brutish and, who would, otherwise be able to slay the poets' fellow soldiers.

The wheels of the limbers crush the bodies which lie on the road. This description of crunching bones is almost disturbingly realistic, leaving nothing to the imagination. The poet points out that in death, there is no difference between friend and enemy, and that in fact, they now lie together. He also implies that as the shells continue over their heads, there will be more deaths to come. The use of the word 'crying' as the noise made by the shells is worth noting, since this would normally be a sound associated with mourners, except of course, these men have no one to mourn them. Rosenberg could also be suggesting that the shells are sorry that these men are dead and are, either genuinely contrite, or are sad because they cannot kill them anymore.

Next he tells us that the earth has been waiting to reclaim these men ever since they were born. He suggests a sense of greed and urgency, almost a blood-lust on the part of the earth, which can only be satisfied and strengthened by a steady supply of the dead.

He seems to believe that the earth has taken the mens' souls and flung their bodies back, leaving them to decay. He questions who has removed the spirits of these men: was it some unseen being -

like a God - or was it the war itself: were these men made soulless by the war, rather than by death. This section of the poem mourns the loss of so many young lives which are described as 'half-used'. It is as though he feels that life has been literally sucked out of these men, like a bee drinking honey. The manner of their deaths is described as 'swift', yet although this implies a lack of suffering, he also seems to be saying that this, almost indecent haste, leaves no time to appreciate their lives, worship their spirits, or mourn their deaths.

Now we return to the living, with an image of Hell. Those still alive are referred to as being thrown onto a funeral pyre, denoting that they are living with the dead. They are able to walk through this scene of devastation as though they are fed and looked after by the Gods, untouched by what lies around them. He seems to suggest that what he is witnessing should be sufficient to make him die from fear, but he has not; so perhaps there is worse still to come. This denotes a sense of immunity to the sights that surround him, and possibly to death itself. He is surrounded by a cacophony of sound - all around him shells burst, as though the sky is raining death. He remembers that those who now lie dead were recently living and 'vigorous'. However, for some, death does not come instantly. The injured, he says, are given time to dream of their home and loved ones and other such things as they have not allowed themselves to ponder, until now. The war and their experiences of it have prevented them from thinking such happy thoughts.

Next comes an image of a stretcher-bearer, whose face is 'splattered' with the brains of the man he is carrying. He puts down the stretcher and when he looks at the wounded soldier again, finds that he is dead. This verse is heart-rending; the language used is simple and very descriptive, so that the reader can picture the stretcher-bearers' brain-splattered face and feel his sense of loss when he realises that the man no longer needs his care. This verse acknowledges that men were still capable of such feelings of caring and kindness, despite their surroundings and experiences.

This dead soldier is left with many others, who have been lying there much longer. The fact that this group of bodies is left at a cross roads is interesting. It could be a literal reference to a cross roads, where bodies are left, hopefully, to be collected and possibly buried; or it might also imply a metaphorical cross roads, where the dead may begin their next journey, presumably to Heaven, while the living return to walk through Hell. These bodies have obviously been lying here for some time as they have turned black with decay - as though they have been burnt. The grass, even the earth itself, appear to have more life in them than these bodies. The physical appearance of these bodies is another reference to Hell and fire.

Amongst the others, there lies the body of a man, who has obviously not been dead for very long. The poet imagines that the man would have heard the wheels of the limber as it approached and how, in desperation he would have reached out, longing for them to stop; or else for his life to end now, since knowing that help was so near and yet being unable to reach it was torture. The description of the dying man crying as life passed from his body, washing over him like a rising tide, even as he still hoped and prayed for help, is deeply moving. The reader can imagine the man's sense of desperation, knowing that help is to hand, while he lies dying and powerless to reach it.

As the limber rounds the bend, the men hear the dying soldier's final cries - literally the last noise he will ever make. Then, as they pass, their wheels, which had given him a final thought of hope, graze his now dead face.

This is amongst the most poignant, brutal and realistic of all First World War poems. By portraying the war as a ceaseless Hell in which hope and youth are lost forever, it is simply and quite unemotionally, stating a fact. Even in the title, Rosenberg has managed to portray this pointless waste, since the dead men are not mourned or buried, but dumped unceremoniously, to rot into the earth, their spirits having long-since been drained by the endless war.

The poignancy of this poem lies in the fact that, without sentimental language, Rosenberg manages to portray pity and sorrow at man's self-destruction. His uncompromising language makes this poem more realistic than many - but without bitterness or anger. Instead his tone is resigned - as though the carnage knows no end and he has already sacrificed himself, safe in the knowledge that the killing will go on. He sees no end in sight, but also does not see a means of justifying what has gone before. He paints an image of a human tragedy unfolding, which there is neither the will nor the power to prevent. In this world, life and death have become confused as have Heaven and Hell, as he is no longer able to distinguish between the two.

This sense of tragic loss and waste is shared by many other poets - notably Siegfried Sassoon, Wilfred Owen and Charles Hamilton Sorley. One poem which bears some comparison with *Dead Man's Dump* is *The Death Bed* by Sassoon, in which he vividly describes the desperation of a dying man, clinging on to life, and the arbitrary nature of death which eventually claims him, despite the fact that he is surrounded by loved ones who are willing him to pull through. Finally, Sassoon reminds us how pointless the young man's battle for life has been, as in the distance, one can still hear the guns.

Sassoon's poem is an intense and beautiful portrayal of the dying man's final thoughts, tempered with the reality of the ongoing war, suggesting that where this young man goes, others will follow - again, as in *Dead Man's Dump*, there is no end in sight. Unlike many of Sassoon's other poems, however, there is no bitterness or blame here, but a powerful description of a young man passing, unwillingly and unfairly, from life to death.

Rosenberg, in *Dead Man's Dump*, gives us an image where life and death are blurred. As in many of his poems, he places himself more with the dead than the living - in this instance on a 'pyre' - a living hell. He portrays the living *and* the dead as spiritless. The life is drained from these men, not yet old enough to have lived and both the dead and the living are left to rot. His language and tone are harsh, not beautiful and even nature is given qualities enabling it to take life: the earth has been eagerly awaiting these dead men - as though through them it gains added strength; the shells are burning bees with a fatal sting; death is like an incoming wave which overpowers the young and consumes them. He is describing, with heart-rending realism, a world which, through its own self-destruction, has gone mad.

SIEGFRIED SASSOON

BIOGRAPHY

Siegfried Loraine Sassoon was born on 8th September 1886 at the family home of Weirleigh at Matfield in Kent. He was the middle of three sons of Alfred and Theresa Sassoon. Alfred was from a wealthy Jewish banking family, but had been disowned by his mother upon his marriage to Theresa, who was not of the Jewish faith. Theresa was a Thornycroft by birth, with an intelligent and artistic nature. She was a strong, independent woman and was very protective of her talented son. Alfred and Theresa separated when Siegfried was five years old and Alfred died four years later of tuberculosis.

Other than these episodes, Siegfried passed a happy and secure childhood, enjoying reading, music, nature and, of course, writing poetry. He was educated at Marlborough and then went on to Clare College, Cambridge, where he studied Law and History, but left without obtaining a degree.

Back at home in Kent, he led a "country squire's" existence of hunting, riding point-to-point races and playing cricket. It was during this time that he was introduced to Edmund Gosse, who became a great influence in Sassoon's early literary career. Siegfried sent Gosse some of his poems and the critic thought well enough of them to show them to Edward Marsh, who was, at that time, Editor of the *Georgian Poetry* anthology. Marsh was impressed and the two men became friends. At Marsh's suggestion, Sassoon moved to London in March 1914 but, despite the obvious advantages of being in London's literary circle, he struggled to maintain his new lifestyle on his limited allowance.

Upon the outbreak of war, Sassoon put his financial worries behind him and immediately enlisted as a Trooper in the Sussex Yeomanry. Siegfried's poetry at this time reflected his limited experiences. A bad fall while riding, however, left Siegfried with a broken arm. When he had recovered from this injury, he transferred to the infantry and was commissioned into the Royal Welch Fusilliers in May 1915.

After training, Siegfried left for France on 24 November 1915 and joined the First Battalion at Béthune. It was at this time that he met fellow poet and Royal Welch Fusillier, Robert Graves.

By now the war had started to become more personal for Siegfried. His younger brother, Hamo, was mortally wounded at Gallipoli and was buried at sea on 1st November 1915. Then on 18th March 1916, his close friend, Second Lieutenant David Thomas was shot in the throat while out with a wiring party, and died of his wound. David Thomas had been an object of great affection for Sassoon, who was moved to write of him in *The Last Meeting*.

These losses had a profound effect on Sassoon and the war became a personal crusade to avenge these deaths. He took to creeping about in front of the British wire, with reckless enthusiasm and soon earned the nickname "Mad Jack". In June his platoon was involved in a raid on Kiel Trench and his selfless actions in retrieving the dead and wounded from No Man's Land earned him the Military Cross. The citation read:

"Owing to his courage and determination, all killed and wounded were brought in".

Sassoon went on to take part in the Battle of the Somme, being recommended for another medal, following a bombing raid. In late July Siegfried became ill with trench fever and was sent home to convalesce. He spent some time with Robert Ross, who had been a close friend of Oscar Wilde. Ross, in turn, introduced Siegfried to Arnold Bennett and HG Wells. Sassoon returned to France in February 1917 but after just two days, was forced into hospital suffering from German measles. Upon returning to the front, ten days later, he joined the Second Battalion, Royal Welch Fusilliers and participated in the Second Battle of the Scarpe, where he was wounded in the shoulder.

Whilst convalescing in England, Sassoon wrote his infamous Declaration, under the influence, it must be said, of prominent pacifists, such as John Middleton Murry and Bertrand Russell. Sassoon's intention in making his Declaration had been a court martial, but this was averted by his friends, including Robert Graves and Edward Marsh.

A medical board (after emotional evidence given by Graves) declared that Sassoon was suffering from shell-shock. Sassoon, who had by now become so disillusioned that he had thrown his medal ribbon into the Mersey river, found himself at Craiglockhart War Hospital, in Edinburgh. The diagnosis of shell-shock was one of convenience for the authorities, desperate to avoid the embarrassment of a courageous and decorated officer, publicly and defiantly opposing the continuation of the war.

During his time at Craiglockhart, Sassoon was treated by Dr W. H. R. Rivers, who came to have a great influence over him and the two men remained close friends until the doctor's death in 1922.

Another, more famous, meeting at this time, was with Wilfred Owen, who was also a patient at Craiglockhart. Sassoon encouraged Owen, in whom he could perceive a genuine and natural talent for writing poetry. He also continued to write many poems himself.

Sassoon suffered from feelings of extreme guilt at being safe at home, while his men were fighting in France, and he took the decision to return to France. On 26th November 1917, he was passed fit for general service.

On 13th February 1918, Sassoon sailed from Southampton and, following a long journey, arrived in Palestine. After three months, in what Sassoon found to be an uncomfortably hot climate, he was glad to be posted back to France. Once settled, Sassoon's foolhardiness re-surfaced and after leading a terrified corporal on a raid into No Man's Land, a euphoric Sassoon stood up in a trench and was shot in the head. He later discovered that he had been shot by one of his own sergeants, who had mistaken him for an advancing German. This wound, while not fatal, was serious enough to mean the end of Siegfried's war and he was placed on indefinite sick leave and eventually retired from the army on 12 March 1919.

In the period immediately following the war, Sassoon met many famous writers, including T.E. Lawrence and Thomas Hardy, with whom Sassoon frequently visited. He also, briefly, became literary editor of the *Daily Herald* and while there received a privately printed volume of poems from Edmund Blunden and through shared interests in poetry and cricket, the two became life-long friends.

Sassoon, in 1928, began writing his autobiographies, initially as a fictionalised account in *Memoirs of a Fox-hunting Man, Memoirs of an Infantry Officer* and finally *Sherston's Progress*, which are collectively known as *The Complete Memoirs of George Sherston*. He then published the non-fiction versions, entitled *The Old Century and Seven More Years, The Weald of Youth* and *Siegfried's Journey*. This is not to say that he ceased writing poetry, but he felt a need to expunge his memories and experiences of the war.

Sassoon's homosexuality, which had remained undiscovered and dormant throughout the war, heightened and he embarked on several romantic adventures, particularly during his travels into Europe during the 1920's. He tired of the fickle nature of these friendships, however, and on 18th December 1933, he married Hester Gatty, daughter of a prominent barrister and the Chief Justice of Gibraltar. In October 1936 Hester and Siegfried had a son, named George. The marriage was not altogether happy. Hester was keen to share her husband's interests and activities, but Sassoon resented her interference and excluded her. They separated in 1945. In 1957, Sassoon was received into the Roman Catholic Church.

Sassoon lived a quiet existence at his home, Heytesbury House in Wiltshire, until his death on September 1st 1967. He is buried at St Andrew's Church at Mells in Somerset.

SASSOON'S WORK

Siegfried Sassoon is probably most famous for his bitter and satirical First World War poetry, and his autobiographical prose.

His pre-war poetry reflected his own loves of hunting and nature, as in, for example *Nimrod in September*. In this poem Sassoon evokes the early morning hunts, which formed a major part of his youth. The autumnal mists and thrill of the hunt are brought to life in a mere eight lines. This is one of Sassoon's greatest abilities - to be descriptive and evocative, yet concise.

When the First World War started, he wrote enthusiastic verse, such as *Absolution*, and after the death of his brother Hamo at Gallipoli, Sassoon wrote *To My Brother* on 18 December 1915. (This poem was originally entitled "Brothers"). Despite the subject matter, this is not an embittered poem; it's tone is sad and reflective and the ending is quite uplifting.

The poem which Sassoon described as his first outspoken war poem was entitled *In The Pink* and was written on 10th February 1916. In this poem Sassoon refers to thoughts of home and whispering to loved ones, and contrasts this with the realities of rotten boots and frozen mud.

One of Sassoon's most quoted early works is *The Kiss*. This was written after a lecture on the bayonet at which Major Campbell (the lecturing officer) had given the bullet and bayonet sibling status. Sassoon refers to the damage these weapons can inflict. In finishing he says he, the soldier, wants the enemy to cower from the bayonet. This could be interpreted in two ways: firstly, he wants the enemy to be afraid and surrender, and thus save him from having to kill them; secondly, he wants to kill the enemy and see their terror before doing so.

The Death Bed was written in August 1916 while Sassoon was convalescing at home. He gives beautiful descriptions of the dying man's surreal sense of floating, and contrasts this with the realism and pain of his death. He speaks of the urgent desperation of all concerned to keep the man alive: which ultimately proves futile and death takes him. Sassoon places this death in context and rouses us from the almost dreamlike quality of the poem with the final line, which serves to remind us that just as this man has died, many more will continue to do so.

They, which was written in October 1916 is a satirical attack on the Establishment - in this instance, the church - and was his attempt to expose the realities of war to those whom Sassoon believed were complacently sitting at home justifying the carnage as a righteous cause.

As the war progressed, Sassoon's poetry became even more bitter as he experienced the needless slaughter of his fellow men. The ultimate effect of this was the writing of his *Declaration*, which criticised not the men who fought, or the conduct of the war, but questioned the validity of the cause, which he claimed had been altered by unimaginative politicians, whose insincerities were resulting in the sacrifice of so many young lives.

His poetry at this time reflected these feelings, as in, for example, *Lamentations*, where he describes the overwhelming and consuming grief of a soldier who has just learned of the death of his brother. Sassoon vividly describes this man's grief - his loss of control - and how this affects those around him. He draws you into this man's suffering and then, with typical Sassoon irony, turns the tables on the reader. Of course, he is not saying he believes it is unpatriotic to grieve but he is trying to force his readers to question their own standards and accept that grief knows no bounds and is universal.

The style of his poems continued in this vein during his stay at Craiglockhart War Hospital, where he wrote, among many others, *Attack*, which describes very evocatively the launching of an assault. He chronicles the final few seconds as these men go over-the-top, demonstrating that while time has, effectively stopped for these men, it continues to pass for others. These men have lost all hope in the drowning mud. He ends with a plaintive and hopeless plea to stop the fighting.

Once Sassoon had decided to leave Craiglockhart and return to the front, he wrote *Banishment*. This poem requires no explanation provided the reader understands Sassoon's perception that his protest against the continuation of the war had failed and that he had recognised a need within himself to return to his men, in order to help them and to share in their hardships and horrors. It also demonstrates that he felt a need to be forgiven by his men for having abandoned them in the first place.

Sassoon continued with his outspoken and frequently bitter poems, but there was also now a more thoughtful and resigned air to his writing. He knew there was nothing that he could do to end the suffering of the men, but that did not lessen his desire to bring it to the attention of the complacent public at home. A perfect example of this is found in *The Dug-Out*, which was written in July 1918, and which describes his fear that the young men around him are going to be permanently affected by what has happened to them, even if they survive. Although the man described is still alive, he might as well be dead.

When the war ended, Sassoon's thoughts turned to *Reconciliation* - the title of a poem he wrote in November 1918, in which he points out that the suffering was universal; that the courageous and loyal German soldiers deserve no less recognition than the British. In March 1919, Sassoon urged us in *Aftermath*, never to forget the suffering and sacrifices of the First World War. He never did.

POETRY ANALYSIS

THE HERO

This poem was written in August 1916. The title is, of course, ironic, in that Jack is not the perceived idea of a hero in the conventional and accepted sense of the time. The first verse deals with the mother's pride when she is told of the heroic nature of her son's death. Despite her obvious grief, she receives great comfort from the knowledge that he died a hero.

In the second stanza, this sentiment is contrasted with the officer's relief at having done his duty, and told the woman of her son's death. He is glad, however, to be able to leave the grieving woman behind.

The third verse reveals the truth: Jack had not died a hero's death. Instead, he had panicked and tried to get himself sent home. The image portrayed of Jack here is of a man who found the war and constant threat of death impossible to cope with and had finally died a needless, unremarkable death.

The language of the final stanza is much more realistic and harsh than the first two, as we learn that Jack was blown to pieces. The description of Jack's fear, and his brutal death, leave nothing to the imagination and this helps to emphasise the differences between the gentle sanctity of the family home and the horrors of the trenches.

The mother's reaction provides the officer with some justification for his falsehood, although his insecurity in his chosen standpoint is obvious from the description of his demeanour. It could be argued that the Brother Officer has, like Jack, shown a cowardly side to his nature - choosing not to tell the old lady the truth and therefore forcing her to live a lie, provides him with an easier solution than being honest with her, and having to deal with the consequences of her shame as well as her grief.

The poem appears, on the surface at least, to sympathise with the mother; but one should always remember Sassoon's capacity for satire. He found the false pride of civilians distasteful; their lack of understanding of the realities faced by the soldiers was a constant thorn in his side. He, therefore, sympathises with her as much for her delusion as for her loss.

The fact that the officer lies not only protects the mother, but also Jack's memory, so it could be argued that Sassoon sympathises, at least in part, with Jack. The representation of Jack seems harsh and unforgiving, but this could, again, be Sassoon's use of irony. Jack's actions should not make him any less worthy of remembrance than those who went blindly into battle, displaying little or no fear. In the end Sassoon points out that his death has gone unnoticed, by everyone except his mother. This would be the accepted reaction of the public to the death of the coward but Sassoon seems to be asking - why should it only be his mother who grieves for him? Is he any less deserving of their thoughts, just because he seems to have lost his nerve? He could also be suggesting that those at home have no right to judge the conduct of a soldier at the front, given their meagre understanding of conditions there.

At the same time as he wrote The Hero, Sassoon also penned The One-Legged Man, which tells of a soldier's relief at being out of the war. He describes how, in coming home, this young man now has the opportunity to live a full life, admire the countryside, find a wife and settle down. In the final line, we learn of the sacrifice which the man has had to make for this peace of mind - he has had a leg amputated. Sassoon, at this time, was vehemently opposed to the glorification of the war and the idea of the "supreme sacrifice", whether it be through death or permanent disfigurement.

It is also possible to compare Sassoon's character, Jack, with Hibbert in *Journey's End* by R. C. Sherriff. Like Jack, Hibbert tries to get sent home and panics at the prospect of being made to continue to fight. Stanhope's reaction as the senior officer is initially harsh, but once he has got Hibbert to see that there is no way out, other than court martial, and death, he empathises with him and lets him know these feelings of fear and foreboding are common - in fact he suffers from them himself. Although he does not like Hibbert as a person, Stanhope's understanding, like Sassoon's demonstrates that many officers could sympathise with those soldiers who found the horrors of war impossible to tolerate.

DOES IT MATTER?

This poem was written while Sassoon was staying at Craiglockhart in 1917 and is possibly influenced by news he had received of two old friends, one of whom had suffered a breakdown and the other who had lost an arm.

This is probably one of Sassoon's most bitter poems, full of irony and cynicism. Sassoon questions whether the permanent disfigurement - both physical and mental - caused by the war, and which affected so many, can be justified in the name of patriotism.

In the first stanza, Sassoon harkens back to his pre-war experiences, such as hunting, which he feels have been lost forever. He points out here, that for someone who has lost their legs, life will never be the same again. Then, with great cynicism, he tells the maimed soldier that he should try not to let anyone else see that he's upset at missing out - and anyway, they will always show him pity - a sentiment which Sassoon would have abhorred.

This is repeated in the second verse, except that this time, the soldier in question has lost his sight. There is a sadness, demonstrated in this stanza, that this soldier, like so many others will only have *memories* of happier days - the future, for him, being bleak and dark.

Finally, Sassoon deals with those who have been mentally scarred by their experiences of the war. Again, he emphasises the piteous way in which the public will look at these men, without ever really trying to understand their situation or their experiences.

It would seem that Sassoon believed that the public were prepared to accept these losses as a just and necessary result of the war. By the use of repeated platitudes Sassoon is trying to shock his readers out of this complacency. He is attempting to induce a sense of impropriety in *their* reactions to the wounded, maimed and scarred.

This poem is often compared to Wilfred Owen's *Disabled*, which tells of the hopeless future faced by an amputee in the war. Sassoon, using simple language and great irony to get his message across, launches a bitter attack on the complacency of civilians, while *Disabled* attempts to point out that this very young (in fact, under-age) soldier has sacrificed more than should rightly be expected. Owen's soldier has forsaken his future, his youth and his chance of happiness and in return, the girls who goaded him into joining up will no longer even look at him.

Sassoon also uses these bitter recriminations in *Glory of Women* which depicts his observation that soldiers were only loved when performing heroic feats or being wounded, and even then only in a place which would not cause any embarrassment. His extreme distaste for this form of hero-worship is self-evident; as is his capacity to see both sides. He switches his thoughts from a British woman who believes the propaganda she is fed, to a German mother, knitting socks for her, already dead, son.

SUICIDE IN THE TRENCHES

Believed to have been written in early 1918, this poem tells the story of a young soldier's mental deterioration and ultimate suicide. The first stanza lulls the reader into a false sense of security. The boy is described as being simple which does not necessarily mean stupid, but should probably be interpreted more as uncomplicated or unpretentious. Sassoon paints a picture of this cheerful young soldier enjoying his humble pleasures and a relatively carefree existence - he sleeps soundly, and wakes early and happily.

In the second verse, however, Sassoon brutally crushes this illusion and describes the effects of the harsh winter and appaling conditions. Being under fire (the word crumps refers to explosions of heavy shellfire) has caused the previously happy and carefree boy to become nervous and depressed. He takes what he sees to be the only way out and kills himself.

The fact that nobody speaks about the suicide can be interpreted as his fellow-soldiers experiencing shame and embarrassment at his action. Alternatively, this silence can be taken as a sense of foreboding and denial. In other words, it seems less real if they don't mention it - they might even be able to pretend that it did not happen at all. Another example of this can be seen in *Journey's End* by R.C. Sherriff where, before the raid, Raleigh and Osborne talk about anything and everything except the war and the raid - choosing to escape, albeit for a few minutes, from the reality of their fate. This silent reaction can also be found in *Spring Offensive* by Wilfred Owen. In this poem, after the battle, the men do not speak of their friends who have died.

Sassoon's anger breaks through in the final stanza, where he berates the crowds, who watch proudly as young soldiers pass. He suggests, with great feeling, that these people should thank God that they have escaped the fate of this young soldier - and many others like him. His definition of the crowd as cowardly and dishonest is interesting as these are not characteristics which he attributes to the dead soldier-boy.

This poem has a lively, simple rhythm which suits the content of the first verse and contrasts with that of verses two and three and, therefore, helps enhance the ironic and angry tone which Sassoon sought to achieve.

BASE DETAILS

In this short, vitriolic poem, Siegfried Sassoon is attacking the senior officers whom he perceives to be responsible for the misconduct of the war. He gives these desk-soldiers an air of unfitness, lack of caring and poor appearance, living as far away as possible from the fighting and danger, yet sending men to their deaths, without a second thought.

This officer sits safely in a hotel, eating and drinking, while perusing the Roll of Honour, commenting on the names that he recognises and how many have been lost in this, most recent, battle. Finally, Sassoon states that the officer, safely away from any fear of death, will - even when all the young men are dead - be able to enjoy the luxury of dying in his own bed.

Base Details is one of Sassoon's most scathing criticisms of the attitude of senior officers. It was written in Rouen in early March 1917, where Sassoon was recovering from a bout of German measles, and reflects a real event which happened while he was there. He had been lunching at the Hôtel de la Poste and had witnessed a Brigadier-General enjoying his meal at a nearby table. The appearance and demeanour of the officer was the inspiration behind this poem.

The title is, in itself, quite interesting since it could have more than one meaning. It could simply mean that what follows is a series of details relating to life at a military base. Equally, it could refer to the base, or humble soldiers, or 'details' as they were also known, and could therefore, demonstrate Sassoon's use of irony. His main concern was always for the welfare of his men, and despite the title, this poem is not about them, but about those who glibly send them to their deaths.

Sassoon puts himself in the position of the officer, but does so conditionally, implying that even he would behave like that *if* he were a senior officer, because that is what they are conditioned to do. However, this is all hypothetical since he is not really a staff officer. The majors are described as scarlet, which may simply mean that they have red faces, probably from consuming excessive quantities of food and alcohol. It may also be a reference to the red shoulder flashes and hat-bands worn by staff officers. Equally, he may be using the word to represent his idea that these men were amoral or unprincipled, like a 'scarlet woman'.

Sassoon describes the ordinary soldiers in heroic terms, but these men do not go happily into battle. Their unhappy appearance is contrasted with that of the officers, who seem to be enjoying their lives. Whilst in his imaginary role as staff officer, Sassoon pictures himself looking at the casualty list until he comes across a familiar name, when he remembers his acquaintance with the father of the named dead soldier. The officer feels no sense of responsibility himself for this, or any of the other deaths on the list and comments blithely on the number of casualties. This demonstrates Sassoon's increasing frustration at the attitude of many non-combatants who claimed an affinity with the soldiers and an understanding of the horrors of the war, while not being expected to participate themselves. His language here demonstrates that he seemed to believe that the staff officers were no better than the civilians, who sat complacently and safely at home. He is also showing his distaste for the army tradition of nurturing, and promoting those who had been to the right school, or knew the right people, regardless of their ability to lead men into battle.

At the end of the poem comes the biting satire, so typical of Sassoon. He imagines himself, still in his role of senior officer, staggering home from the war, and the death of a generation, for which he is responsible, to die in the comfort and security of his own bed. In these final two lines, Sassoon's officer is portrayed as satisfied at the outcome of the war, although there is no mention of victory. This is because, for Sassoon, there were no winners - everyone lost, because the human cost of the war had proved to be too high a price, even for the 'victorious'.

The officer is likened to a young child, toddling home to the sanctity of his own bed, where he will have the satisfaction of dying peacefully. This is not a comfort which has been afforded to the ranks of soldiers for whose deaths he is responsible. Sassoon's implication here is that the officer deserves such a death less than anyone else.

This poem is typical of many, which Sassoon wrote at around this time, such as *The General* and *Lamentations*. The ultimate outcome of this was Sassoon's Declaration which he wrote in the summer of 1917. He always felt very strongly about the treatment of the ordinary soldiers who were expected to fight and die for their country. The senior officers, on the other hand, were professional soldiers, who should, Sassoon felt, have shown more understanding and compassion for those whose lives they were sacrificing.

LAMENTATIONS

This satirical poem reads like a narrative of a scene, describing a man's profound grief, with any opinion reserved for the very last sentence. The narrator - in all probability an officer - hears the sound of a man crying as he wanders down a dark corridor. This area is so dark, in fact, that nothing can be distinguished except the sound of crying - the noise dominates all other senses to the point where they no longer seem to function. The officer clumsily enters the room: he does not peer around the door to see what is happening, but stumbles in upon the scene. This may be because Sassoon is subtly pointing out, right from the beginning, that the officer has a air of arrogance about him.

The crying man is not alone: there is a sergeant standing nearby watching him. He makes no attempt to pacify the man, but we are informed that this would be pointless. The man is too upset, it would seem, to listen to reason. Interestingly, although no-one could hope to calm him in his present state, they offer him no comfort either - they merely stand and observe, almost as though the crying man is so alien to them that they have no idea how to react.

There follows the first hint of irony as we are informed that the 'only' reason for the man's behaviour is that his brother has died. The implication here is that the receipt of such news is a poor excuse for behaving in this manner, but this is delivered with such an air of incredulity that the reader can easily understand Sassoon's use of satire. The description of the man's grief demonstrates that he has lost control of his feelings. The use of such emotive language in this passage makes his reaction more realistic and enables the reader to sympathise with the grieving man, whose emotions have obviously, and understandably, become overwhelming.

Finally, Sassoon launches his satirical attack by implying that this man's behaviour is not merely unacceptable: it is unpatriotic. He ironically implies that in order to be considered a true patriot, men must hide their feelings and their grief and think only of 'the cause', regardless of any personal sacrifices which may be required of them.

This poem was written in the summer of 1917, but is based on an episode which Sassoon witnessed while he was at the Infantry Base Depot at Rouen. He arrived there on 16th February 1917, on his way back to the front, having been on leave following an attack of trench fever. Sassoon was actually searching for a storeroom when he found himself in the guardroom instead, witnessing this scene, exactly as he describes it in this poem. The man in question had been under detention for striking a military police officer, when he had been told the news about his brother. Sassoon received this explanation from the sergeant who seemed surprised at the strength of the man's reaction - even to the point of wondering if he was suffering from shell-shock.

The title of the poem is interesting: a lamentation is a passionate demonstration of grief, and as such describes the man's reaction perfectly. However, there is another explanation for this title: the book of *Lamentations* in the Bible which is, essentially, a series of five poems, offering a reflection on the handling of grief. The language used in describing the act of grieving is similar, and this may also be interpreted as Sassoon criticising (not for the first time) the attitude of the church towards the war. In other words, he could be expressing the opinion that if people in the Bible are allowed to beat their chests, wail and sob uncontrollably, why cannot those who are grieving during the War behave in a similar fashion: why must *they* hide their feelings?

In common with many of Sassoon's satirical verses, he initially sets about creating an atmosphere, which in this instance leads the reader to sympathise with the grieving man, whose emotions are laid bare. The description given of his physical reaction to the death of his brother is very evocative. In typical Sassoon style, having captivated the imagination of the reader, the real message of the poem is saved until the end and is delivered in a satirical tone. The narrator, we learn, has no sympathy for this man, contemptuously stating that his behaviour demonstrates his lack of patriotism.

Sassoon often used satire in this way to show his own contempt for the attitudes of others. A good example of this can be seen in *They* where his target is the church, or more specifically, the clergy, whose platitudes on the justness of the war angered Sassoon. In this instance, although the bishop is allowed the last word, this is only done to illustrate the predictable, banal nature of his comments.

Later in the summer of 1917, Sassoon wrote *How to Die* which looks at death from the perspective of the dying soldier rather than the grieving relative. In this poem, he points out that the men have a responsibility to die tastefully, and with propriety while not making any unnecessary fuss. In the first verse, he offers a description of a man dying at dawn in a shell-hole, with the name of a loved-one being his last whispered utterance. Next he suggests that the dying, contrary to popular belief, do not cry or scream, or long for glorious remembrances and memorials, because they have been taught to die properly, almost as though this were a necessary part of their training.

Both *How to Die* and *Lamentations* show the de-humanising effects of the war: feelings must be repressed; men must behave like men; everyone must remember what they are fighting for; maintenance of morale is of the highest importance, so there should not be too much emphasis on death.

Although some may argue that Sassoon took his arguments to an extreme, he was, by this stage of the war, extremely angry. He had witnessed too much suffering at the front, too much unfeeling arrogance amongst some of the senior officers and too much complacency at home to sit back and say nothing. He wanted to shock others into seeing, and understanding the brutal realities of war, death and grief. By the time these poems were published in June 1918, a significant number of people were beginning to agree with him.

THE DUG-OUT

This poem was written in July 1918 and was based on one of Sassoon's final experiences in the trenches before he was wounded and eventually invalided out of the Army. He and a subaltern, named Jowett, had been out on patrol and upon their return, the exhausted Jowett had collapsed into a dug-out, sound asleep. Sassoon, seeing him lying there in a huddled position, had thought him reminiscent of a corpse.

The Dug-Out clearly demonstrates Sassoon's passionate feelings towards his colleagues at the front, many of whom he physically admired. It is easy to imagine Sassoon, who was by this time a company commander, standing in the doorway of the dug-out admiring the younger man, sleeping in the dim candlelight. He obviously sympathises with the junior officer, who is cold, unhappy and extremely tired. These were common complaints among both officers and men, particularly at this late stage of the war.

Sassoon describes how miserable he feels, watching the young man's face in the shadows, and so he wakes him up, just to convince himself that he's still alive. This demonstrates how, by this stage of the war, Sassoon - like many others - had grown so used to death surrounding him and intruding on every aspect of his life, that he finds it necessary to rouse this young officer, purely for the purpose of reassuring himself. This part of the poem also shows how Sassoon, and many other officers, represented a parental figure to their men - having to be both mother and father in many cases. Officers had to take care of many aspects of their men's lives, from arranging billets and food, to ensuring that kit and weapons were properly looked after. In waking the sleeping officer, Sassoon becomes reminiscent of a parent checking that their sleeping child is safe.

It is worth remembering that, by the time he wrote this poem, Sassoon would have been nearly 32 years old, and therefore, his age and experience would have made him appear as even more of a father-figure to his men than many other, younger officers. He had always felt responsible for the welfare of his men, as well as extremely angry at the waste of so many young lives. To Sassoon, all of his men would have seemed too young to die, and any death would be deemed by him to be unnecessary.

This is one of Sassoon's most sympathetic poems - there is no satire or irony here, because The Dug-Out is directed at someone Sassoon really cares about - rather than someone at whom he would be directing anger or criticism. Although there is nothing explicitly homo-erotic in this poem, there are definite undertones of admiration and regret. Sassoon's sexuality at this stage of his life was a source of great difficulty for him: he found some of the men with whom he was serving physically attractive - even beautiful - yet was fully aware of the implications of a serving officer being discovered to be homosexual.

There is a soft, mellow, hushed tone and a relaxed, unhurried atmosphere in this poem, which is reminds us of the sleeping officer, but also lulls the reader into the same mental state. Although concerned about the sleeping man, Sassoon's questioning of his welfare is not done in a hurried or panicking manner, which adds to this mood of exhaustion and resignation.

CHARLES HAMILTON SORLEY

BIOGRAPHY

Charles Sorley was born on May 19, 1895 in Aberdeen where his father, William Ritchie Sorley taught at the University. At the age of five, Charles, his twin brother and his older sister, moved to Cambridge when their father took up the position of Professor of Moral Philosophy at the University.

The twins both attended King's College Choir School and then in 1908, Charles, an uncommonly intelligent boy, won a scholarship to Marlborough College. While there, Sorley developed an interest in cross-country running which enabled him to enjoy the Wiltshire countryside. He was also keen on debating and writing poetry.

In 1913, Sorley won a scholarship to Oxford, but decided to take a year out and go travelling. January 1914 found him in Mecklenburg in Germany, where he acquired a great admiration for the German people and their culture.

By the end of July 1914, it had become clear that relations between Great Britain and Germany were heading towards conflict and Professor Sorley wrote to his son urging his prompt return. Unfortunately, Charles was on a walking tour, so his receipt of this letter was delayed. On 3rd August he was arrested and imprisoned. This incarceration was brief, lasting a mere eight hours and upon his release he left Germany and returned to England.

Although, as a Scot, Sorley was not especially patriotic towards England, he was keen to enlist and initially formed the notion of putting his socialist ideals into practice and joining up as a private soldier. Eventually, however, he accepted a commission into the Suffolk Regiment. On 26th August he was gazetted as a Temporary Second Lieutenant in the 7th Battalion.

He was sent out to France following training, in May 1915, serving in the Ypres Salient. During this time, he took part in many raids and began to become more hardened - expressing in a letter home his profound relief that a wounded man who was with him in No Man's Land had died, thus obviating the necessity of carrying the man back to the trenches. His relief was not borne out of selfishness, more from his revulsion at having to carry someone who was now little more than flesh and bone.

In August he was promoted to the rank of Captain. September saw the beginning of the Battle of Loos - a disastrous attack which resulted in over 50,000 British casualties. The British, having initially failed to make any headway, re-launched the attack on 13th October, and Sorley's battalion moved into the front line at the Hohenzollern Redoubt, during the previous day.

On Wednesday October 13th Sorley was shot in the head and killed instantly. He was twenty years old. In the bitter fight that followed, his body was not recovered and he is commemorated on the Loos Memorial to The Missing at Dud Corner Cemetery.

Many of his poems were found in his kitbag and his father arranged for their publication under the title *Marlborough and Other Poems* in January 1916.

Charles Hamilton Sorley soon became a favourite with other poets, particularly Robert Graves who regarded the loss of this talented young man as a waste.

POETRY ANALYSIS

ALL THE HILLS AND VALES ALONG

This poem is, in some cases called *Route March*, but it would seem that Sorley himself left it untitled, so it has adopted its first line as a title.

Written shortly after the outbreak of the First World War, this poem could be interpreted as a celebration of death in the sense that re-joining with the earth should be man's ultimate ambition. Its rhyming couplets and jaunty style give it the air of a happy marching song, which contrasts well with the content. Sorley's use of language reinforces this - the subject matter is death, but he uses the word glad or gladness seven times during the poem, and the words joyful and merry also appear on several occasions. This is a poem about the ranks, not the officers: the private soldiers would have sung on the march up to the front; the officers would not.

The first verse sets the tone for the rest of the poem - the men should be glad to give their lives back to the earth, which will be happy to receive them. In the second stanza, Sorley urges the men to consider what lies ahead. He implies that the manner and length of their lives are unimportant compared to the manner of their deaths. He compares this with Christ and Barabbas. Barabbas was the condemned prisoner who was chosen by the Jews to be released, thus sending Christ to die on the cross. The implication here is that death is indiscriminate: the best, most worthy will not necessarily be the ones to survive; but if all men go gladly to their death, the earth will be able to store up all their happiness, as though it were goodness, and this will in turn replenish the earth. This reiterates the first line of this stanza, where he suggests the men should forget about past sins - for in death all will be treated equally.

In the third verse, Sorley talks of the earth only knowing death and not tears, meaning that the earth will not mourn those who will die. In fact, he says, it was the earth that with easy pleasure grew the hemlock with which the Greek philosopher Socrates was killed. This joyous, unlamenting earth, in fact, he says, continued to blossom at the foot of Christ's cross. It will, therefore, continue to flourish when you, the soldier, are dead.

In the final verse, there is an air of celebration where Sorley seems to believe that the earth is laughing and echoing the sounds of the men. This echo, Sorley implies, will continue, even when the singing and marching have all stopped. The final, rousing, section urges the men on to die happily.

This poem is not patriotic: nowhere does it mention the country from which these soldiers come. This was fairly unusual for poetry written at this time, which tended to be full of patriotism, but there is evidence that during his stay in Germany, Sorley had witnessed some German soldiers singing. This, together with hearing the British soldiers' marching songs, may have prompted the writing of this poem.

Sorley makes no mention of his own death: this is not a poem which talks about sacrifice or waste. The men are not dying for King or Country, nor for their fellow man, but for their love of the "earth"; of nature. Unlike in Julian Grenfell's *Into Battle*, the men will not be enlarged by death, but the earth will; there is no joy in Sorley's battle, just the sure inevitability of death.

To Sorley, though, death is not the end. Twice during the poem he says that the men are only sleeping; he talks of the earth storing their gladness, which implies that it will be there for them to return

to later. There is a sense that, to Sorley, death is seen as a fresh
beginning; a reawakening.

WHEN YOU SEE MILLIONS OF THE MOUTHLESS DEAD

This untitled poem, was among those found in Sorley's kitbag after his death. Many critics recognise it in, an awareness and talent which, had he lived, could have rivalled that of Wilfred Owen. This could be said to be true of the form and language, particularly given this poem's nightmarish quality. Sorley's sonnet, however, urges us *not* to praise or mourn the dead, while Owen extols their virtues, particularly when compared to those who mourn them. Owen often uses bitter recrimination as in, for example, *Apologia Pro Poemate Meo* in which he states his opinion that the dead are infinitely more worthy than those whom they have left behind.

Another interesting point which immediately strikes the reader in Sorley's sonnet is the quantity of dead people he envisages. Bearing in mind that this poem was written some time before October 1915, Sorley is showing remarkable foresight and accuracy in his prediction that there will be millions of dead.

There is a shadowy, ethereal quality to Sorley's sonnet: the pale soldiers which march through your dreams lead us into the poet's idea of how one should mourn the dead. This is given in the form of a list of instructions.

Sorley informs us that we need not promise to remember them. He says there is no point in praising them, or crying over them. Neither should we honour them. The reason for all of this is that, being dead, they are deaf, blind and indeed mute - hence "mouthless" - so they can neither appreciate, understand or respond to our sentiments.

He then urges us to appreciate that, although our loved-ones may be dead, many other, equally deserving, men have died before. The dead are no longer exclusively ours to mourn and we should not think of them in this way, or imagine that we are able to recognise them among all the countless others. Death has taken possession of them.

As well as being compared to some of Wilfred Owen's work, many have also seen this sonnet as a response to Rupert Brooke's *The Soldier*. Sorley had been critical of some of Brooke's work, paying particular attention to his obsession with his own sacrifice, and sentimental attitude. As in *All the Hills and Vales Along*, there is no use of the first person in this poem: Sorley talks about the war and death as though they affect others, not himself.

Another parallel could be drawn between this poem and Laurence Binyon's *For The Fallen*. This poem, part of which is read out every year at Remembrance Day services, was first published in September 1914, so it is not unreasonable to suppose that Sorley might have read it. Binyon asserts that we will (and indeed should) remember the dead on a daily basis, and also that their youth is eternal. Sorley, on the other hand, is more blunt: remembering the dead is pointless - they cannot appreciate it, and they are not eternally young, they are dead.

There is no trace of sentimentality in this sonnet, which looks quite harshly at the reality of death through war, making, unlike Brooke and Binyon, no allowance for patriotism or emotion.

EDWARD THOMAS

BIOGRAPHY

Born in London on 3rd March 1878, Philip Edward Thomas was the eldest of six sons. His parents, although originally from Wales, classified themselves as Londoners. Edward grew up in various parts of London, including Lambeth, Wandsworth, Clapham and Balham, but due to frequent holidays spent in Wales and Wiltshire, he soon developed a life-long interest in nature and the countryside.

Edward attended various Board and Independent schools before being enrolled at St Paul's in Hammersmith at the age of fifteen. In many ways, he was a typical Edwardian schoolboy who, by today's standards, could appear harsh. His image, during his schooldays, was that of a loner who felt himself to be superior to his fellow students (particularly while he attended Board school), due to his father's position as a civil servant at the Board of Trade.

At this time, Thomas came under the influence of the essayist, editor and critic James Ashcroft Noble who encouraged his writing and urged him to send his essays to the 'weeklies' for publication. Edward, who, despite a natural shyness, had always had an affinity with women, also met and fell in love with Noble's daughter, Helen.

At the age of twenty, on 4th October 1898, Edward took up his place at Lincoln College, Oxford. Despite missing Helen terribly, he embarked keenly on university life, becoming an avid rower, while still enjoying long walks in the countryside, which had always been, and would remain, a constant feature of his life. He returned home to Helen during the Easter holidays on 1899 and it was at this time that their first child was conceived. Once Helen's pregnancy became known to the couple, they decided to marry, and did so in a small, secretive service on 20th June 1899 at Fulham Registry Office. Their only son, Merfyn, was born on 15th January 1900.

Thomas graduated from Oxford later that year and decided, against his father's wishes, to become a writer. The young family lived initially in London, but Edward was drawn to the countryside and in 1901 they moved to Maidstone in Kent. A year later, their first daughter, Bronwen, was born. Thomas's choice of career had resulted in the family living in dire financial circumstances until he gained employment as the literary reviewer for *The Daily Chronicle*. Although this was not a well-paid position, it at least gave Edward a regular income.

Edward, Helen and their two young children moved several times before settling in Petersfield in Hampshire at the end of 1906. Helen taught in the Kindergarten at nearby Bedales School, which was also attended by both children. In August 1910, a second daughter, Myfanwy, was born, thus completing Edward's family.

Despite ill health, exhaustion and bouts of depression, Edward continued to write reviews and biographies, frequently travelling to London, as well as visiting and walking through many beautiful areas of England, writing nature essays and books. His depressive mood swings forced repeated absences from the family home, but Helen's love for him remained constant. Edward was always torn between his perceived traditional role as a provider for his family and his desire to spend solitary time researching and developing his writing.

In November 1912, Edward met Eleanor Farjeon who became a close friend and frequent visitor to the Thomas family home, as well as a valued critic of his poetry. She also undertook the task of typing out his manuscripts and sending them off to publishers, all of whom rejected them. Eleanor was in love with Edward, but she never revealed this to him, since she was aware of his deep devotion to Helen, and feared that such a declaration would end their friendship.

An even greater influence in Edward's life came almost a year later, when he was first introduced to the American poet, Robert Frost. He encouraged Thomas to write poetry and the two families spent a great deal of time together.

When war was declared in August 1914, Thomas was under no obligation to enlist, since he was too old. He considered many options, including returning to America with the Frosts, before deciding to enlist in the Artists Rifles in July 1915. Eleanor Farjeon noted, at this time, that, having made this decision, he seemed greatly relieved and less tormented than she had ever known him. He had come to believe, quite literally, that he was fighting for the very essence of England.

Thomas spent several weeks as a map-reading instructor at Hare Hall Camp before being commissioned as a Second Lieutenant and posted to the Royal Garrison Artillery. He embarked for France on the 29th January 1917, by which time all of his 144 poems had already been written. He had said his final goodbyes to Helen on 11th January, leaving her desolate and wondering how she would cope without him. During his time at the Front, he wrote regular letters home and Helen lived in the hope of him returning safely, as he had promised he would.

On Easter Sunday 1917, Thomas wrote a happy letter to Helen, in which he described the joyous sounds of hedge sparrows, which he had managed to discern in between the noise of the shellfire and guns. In the same post as this letter, Helen received news from one of Edward's brother officers, giving her details of the event she had long dreaded: Edwards death from a shell-blast on Easter Monday, 9th April 1917.

Helen was, understandably, devastated to receive news of Edward's death, as was Eleanor Farjeon who at Helen's request stayed with the young widow and her children for a few weeks, helping where she could with household duties and in looking after the children. Eleanor was deeply affected by the sight of Helen's grief and this made her appreciate, more than ever, that the war was shattering, irrevocably, the lives of so many people.

Edward Thomas is buried at Agny Military Cemetery, in the Pas de Calais, France. His name is one among fifteen other war poets, engraved on a large commemorative stone in Poet's Corner in Westminster Abbey.

Critical acclaim for Edward Thomas's work was slow in coming, despite Helen's efforts to bring it to the public's attention following his death. Over more recent years, however, his poetry has come to be regarded as an honest and sincere reflection of a talented poet and his time, his beloved countryside and a way of life which would soon be lost forever.

POETRY ANALYSIS

AS THE TEAM'S HEAD-BRASS

The title of this poem, and its first line refer to a team of horses, ploughing a field and the glint created by the sun catching their bridles as they turn back and forth. This team of horses could also be an allusion to the horses at the front, who would have pulled artillery and supply carts through the muddy battlefields.

The narrator notices a couple disappear into the woods in the distance. The first two lines of this poem are symbolic of continuing life: the horses ploughing the field denote the beginning of another year of growth; the lovers going into the woods, presumably for some clandestine affair, demonstrate nature's rebirth. It could be noted, however, that the lovers mentioned are not necessarily people: Edward Thomas often referred to animals and birds as "making love", thus giving them an almost human quality.

The narrator tells us that he is sitting in the branches of an elm tree, which has fallen across the furrows in a section of the field that has already been ploughed. This fallen tree could be a reference to the fallen soldiers in France, who lie in barren fields, just like this one being ploughed. From here he watches the remainder of the ploughing. Charlock is a weed of the mustard family with bright yellow flowers: therefore the field appears to be turning from yellow to brown as it is ploughed, just as the plants, trees and flowers in France have been destroyed. The choice of yellow as a colour provides an internal rhyme pattern with the words "fallen" and "fallow" from the previous two lines.

Each time the horses approach him, as they plough monotonously up and down the field, the narrator fears that he will be run-down, but the ploughman pauses sufficiently each time to exchange a few words, before turning the horses and working his way back up the field. It is as though, by sitting on the dead tree, the narrator (and the reader) fear that he has some affinity with the fallen. Initially the two men talk about the weather, but then their conversation turns towards the war. The ploughman scrapes the blade of his plough as he turns the horses back towards the woods. This also reminds the reader of the blades being used to kill the soldiers at the Front.

The narrator learns that the elm was felled by a heavy snowstorm. This serves as a reminder of the many soldiers who must have died during the cold winters, as though they too have been "felled" by the weather. He asks the ploughman when the tree will be removed and is informed that this will not occur until after the war has finished. Again, there could be said to be a similarity between the tree and the dead soldiers, who will not have proper graves (or in many cases will not have a grave at all) until the war is over. Many dead soldiers were left in No Man's Land and have no known grave, or remained there until the fighting had died down sufficiently for their bodies to be recovered. This conversation between the two men is broken by a gap of ten minutes every time the ploughman turns to plough another length of the field.

The ploughman enquires whether the narrator has served in the war. When he receives a negative answer, he suggests that the man might be avoiding service. The narrator replies that he would happily go if only he knew that he would definitely be coming back. He says that he feels he would not mind losing an arm, but to lose a leg would be a different matter altogether. It is quite likely that Thomas, himself, felt this way - for him the prospect of no longer being able to enjoy his long walks in the countryside would have made life seem intolerable. Death, on the other hand, would be more favourable, since he would no longer want for, or worry about, anything.

The narrator asks whether many men from the surrounding area have gone to the front and died. The ploughman informs him that one of his work-mates had been killed the previous March. In fact, he says, the man was killed on the very night of the blizzard which felled the elm tree. This again reiterates the similarity between the fallen tree and the dead soldiers. The ploughman believes that if his friend had not gone to the front and been killed, the tree would by now have been removed. This indicates that, for those not directly affected by death, life carries on much as before.

However, if the tree had been removed, the narrator should not have been able to sit there and have this conversation. In fact, he says, everything would be different without the war. The ploughman believes that, in that case, the world would be a better place. He then decides that, provided everyone could come back alive, everything might be alright. The word "might" is important here since it demonstrates the doubt in the ploughman's mind, that their world will ever be "alright" again.

As the plough turns one last time, the lovers leave the wood, reminding us once more that, for some, life *is* continuing. The narrator watches the plough work its way through the field. The churning of the mud, once more, brings to mind the muddy battlefields: the uneven tread of the horses and the ploughman call to mind the stumbling and dying soldiers.

This poem continually uses imagery of light and dark: the brass glints in the sunlight; the yellow charlock also represents the sun, light and life which are being cut down by the plough. The woods speak of darkness, since we cannot know what happens in there. The earth also symbolises the dark, in both its colour, its reminiscence of the battlefields and the image of the earth as a grave.

In addition, we are constantly reminded of the images of birth (or life) and death. The very ploughing of the field itself represents the potential birth of new crops, while also bringing about the death of the weeds. The weeds themselves embody plants which serve no purpose - they are deemed useless. This could be equated with the idea that those dying in the war, are being cut down for no reason - their deaths serving no useful purpose. The lovers entering the woods, whether they are human lovers or not, epitomise the suggestion that life goes on as before, and that for some, it will continue to do so, with or without the war.

This poem represents two sides of nature: the death and destruction of war on one side; the continuity of life and the strength of nature itself on the other.

Towards the end of the poem, the ploughman introduces a note of optimism that all *might* be well; this is short-lived since the narrator feels that everything is being done for the last time. The language used at the end of the poem is down-beat: "crumble", "topple over" and "stumbling", all of which denote finality. *As the Team's Head-Brass* was written while Thomas was trying to decide whether or not to apply for a commission and go overseas to serve, and as such, it reflects his uncertainty about the future.

During his time as a map-reading instructor, he had found himself with less and less time to enjoy his walks in the countryside, which may have led him to reflect on how his life would change should he find himself physically maimed and unable to pursue this activity again. He also worried about the future for his family, should the worst happen. Thomas looked upon his role in the family very traditionally and feared for Helen and his children's security should he not return.

Edward Thomas found it difficult to compare his war-time persona and responsibilities with his peace-time ones and possibly had difficulty contemplating the future in the knowledge that his old world and values would probably have disappeared for ever. Even if he survived, so many others would be dead, that his beloved England, and a way of life he had come to depend upon, might never recover.

The conversational tone of this poem could be compared and contrasted with other poems, such as *Comrades: An Episode* by Robert Nichols, or *They* by Siegfried Sassoon. Both Nichols and Thomas use conversation as a means of telling a story and creating a scene, whereas Sassoon is more likely to use it to demonstrate the personality of someone involved. He also uses speech as a way of reinforcing irony with directly-spoken sarcasm.

Unlike Nichols, however, Thomas's conversation is not between soldiers, but civilians. *Comrades: An Episode* is set in a trench and in No Man's Land, and deals with the relationships between soldiers serving at the front. Conversely, *As the Team's Head Brass* uses rural England as its location, and deals, fundamentally with the relationship between man and nature. This reflects the poet's concern for his native country by creating a scene which he fears will soon cease to exist.

THIS IS NO CASE OF PETTY RIGHT OR WRONG

This poem opens with the affirmation that the war is not so simple as the rhetoric of the politicians and philosophers would have us believe. Thomas appears to criticise those who are attempting to heighten nationalistic fervour by creating a hatred and distrust of the German people as a whole. He sees the guilty parties here as the newspapers, and those who spout patriotism, while doing nothing to help the country themselves - thus their indolence has made them "fat" or complacent.

He tells us that he feels more hatred towards these so-called patriots, who are in fact more like parasites sucking the life out of the nation, than he does towards the Kaiser himself. He seems to believe that the Kaiser has almost deified himself, and calls his nation to arms to protect *their* way of life.

Then he points out that it is not his place to decide between the corpulent patriots and the Kaiser. He feels as though he has been deafened by the clamour of war, and cannot make sense of any more of the arguments for or against. He feels confused and compares this confusion with trees in a storm, surrounded by the blowing, howling wind and unable to escape from the cacophony.

Into all this seemingly endless noise, he adds the "roar" of witches' cauldrons. This could be an allusion to *Macbeth* by William Shakespeare, in which the witches first appear in the midst of a terrible thunderstorm and speak of meeting with Macbeth "when the hurlyburly's done,/When the battle's lost and won." These witches can predict the future and although their initial tidings for Macbeth appear promising, their fulfilment ultimately brings about his downfall. Thomas's cauldrons predict a rosy future, fair and beautiful, yet he reminds us that in order to bring about this idyllic image, the old England must die.

Thomas says that he does not care whether, in the future, historians are able to fathom a reason for the conflict, as, by that stage, England - unsurpassed in beauty - will have risen from the ashes of self-destruction and be serene once more. Such serenity has a greater value to Thomas than the historian's knowledge or understanding. He is implying that the reasons for the war, are themselves, unimportant.

The poet states that he stands, as one, with every true Englishman, in his desire to save his country, for such a loss could never be recovered. It is as though he believes himself to be joined with his country and he is comforted by his familiarity with it and by its innate goodness. He avers that if such a love for one's country and a desire to protect it necessitate a hatred of the enemy, then so be it: for as much as he does not love all Englishmen, or hate all Germans, his love for England and wish for its preservation is paramount. It is worth noting that he does not perceive the enemy as *his* enemy, but England's.

Written at the end of 1915, after Thomas had enlisted, this poem was, almost certainly, a means of justifying (even if only to himself) his decision to enter the war. He feels that the necessity to defeat the enemy and protect his beloved England, is more important than any protestations of politicians, philosophers, journalists or historians.

This poem could also be interpreted as a criticism of the more jingoistic poets and writers, whose calls to arms were regularly published at this time. He had, at one stage, been publicly critical of Rupert Brooke's poems, accusing him of arrogance and self-promotion. This, despite the fact that he and Brooke had both been members of the small band of Georgian poets, known as the Dymock Group, demonstrates that to Thomas, the war was not about men and deeds, but about preserving the future of England.

The tone of this poem, like much of Thomas's work, is patriotic and is, in some ways, similar to Julian Grenfell's *Into Battle*. Both poems praise the idea of protecting one's country and fighting for what is held dear. In contrast to Thomas's poem, however, Grenfell writes very much from a soldier's perspective: a soldier, that is, who firmly believes in the righteousness of his cause. Grenfell had little time for those who would not fight, believing them to be as good as dead. *Into Battle* affirms Grenfell's belief that those who die fighting for their country and for what they believe in, will, of necessity, be greater and better than those who refuse to fight. Thomas does not seem to agree with this philosophy. To him the heroic nature of the deed is of minimal importance compared to the continuation of the way of life which he holds so dear.

This poem has a more optimistic tone than *As the Team's Head Brass*. Here there are fewer negative images, England being portrayed as virtuous and beautiful, and worthy of salvation.

A PRIVATE

The title of this poem is interesting since it gives the nameless subject anonymity - he could be any one of the thousands of dead privates currently lying in unknown graves in France.

The subject being a ploughman is representative of Thomas's beloved countryside - a common theme in his poetry which is repeated in the later poem *As the Team's Head Brass*. We are informed very early in this poem that the soldier is dead, which, together with the representation of frosty nights gives the beginning of the poem a cold and almost depressing edge. Then we learn that, in life this man was merry which contrasts with the earlier impression and causes great feelings of regret that one so happy should now be dead.

Whilst at home in England, the ploughman had often slept out of doors, despite the cold and when asked by anyone where he slept, would respond that he slept in a specific hawthorn bush. Interestingly, the bush is given a proper name, while the ploughman is not, showing that to Thomas, the countryside is as important (if not more so) as the people who reside in it. Nobody ever knew where this bush was, implying that the man may have invented this place, so as to keep his real hideaway a secret. In fact, we learn, the downs above the town are filled with many such bushes, any one of which might be hiding a sleeping countryman.

Thomas tells us the name of the pub in which the ploughman used to drink, thus removing *some* of his anonymity, giving him a more human quality and, therefore, forcing us to care even more about his death. We are finally reminded that this serene image of country life is now spoiled because the ploughman went to war, became a private and gave his life. He lies somewhere in France, but, as in life, his exact whereabouts are a secret. Like many of the dead, he - as yet - has no known grave.

This poem was written early in 1915, possibly while Thomas was recovering from a severely sprained ankle, and regretting his missed opportunity to travel to America with Robert Frost. He was, at this stage, still undecided as to whether or not to enter the war.

Unlike many of Thomas's other poems, this is not overtly patriotic, and although he creates an idyllic scene of the Wiltshire countryside, he makes no mention of preserving England and her ways and beauty. Instead, this poem is more a celebration of the simple country folk who have gone to war and will not return. His love for the countryside still shines through as he praises the honesty, serenity and courage of these men who have, without great clamour or fuss, given everything for their country.

COMPARISONS - A GUIDE

Students are frequently asked to make comparisons between poems by either the same or different poets. At first, this can seem a daunting task, but with practice it can become easier.

Obviously, the poems you will be asked to compare could be wide ranging and different and it would, therefore, be impossible for any Study Guide to provide an analysis for you. Here, however, are a few tips to help you when making comparisons.

Firstly, read both the poems through and analyse each of them as described on page nine of this Study Guide. Once you feel you have a good understanding of the poems, start to make a list of similarities and differences. Pay particular attention to themes, language and form.

If the two poems are giving opposing viewpoints, as in Jessie Pope's *Who's For The Game* and Wilfred Owen's *Dulce Et Decorum Est*, then the differences are obvious, but ask yourself are there any similarities? Do they, for example, use the same type of language?

On the other hand, the two poems may be more similar - either in content or language, so now you must look for the differences. If the language is the same, is the content different? For example, you may have two nature poems, one of which is showing the war as destructive, while the other demonstrates a more glorious viewpoint.

In making comparisons, you should always try to show differences *and* similarities. Bear in mind that the poems selected will invariably demonstrate both - your task is to discover these, illustrate your understanding and provide evidence by drawing on quotations from the text to validate and support your interpretations.

FURTHER READING

Poems of the First World War - Never Such Innocence
Edited by Martin Stephen
Probably one of the best anthologies of First World War poetry.
Contains poems by the better known soldier-poets as well as some
more obscure, or indeed, unheard of ones.

Out in the Dark - Poetry of the First World War in Context and with Basic Notes
Edited by David Roberts
Using letters, diaries and contemporary comments this excellent
reference book studies the effect of the war on those who were
writing about it at the time.

Minds at War - The Poetry and Experience of the First World War
Edited by David Roberts
A similar book to Out in the Dark, but with additional notes and
more detailed biographical information for the advanced student.

Anthem for Doomed Youth
by Jon Stallworthy
Excellent and accessible information on twelve poets of the great
war which includes biographical detail and analysis of some of their
works.

The Great War and Modern Memory
by Paul Fussell
The definitive guide to the literature of the period.

1914: The Days of Hope
by Lyn MacDonald
Using diary extracts and first-hand accounts, Lyn MacDonald brings to life the first few months of the First World War. Reading this book should enable students to understand better the attitude of the war poets.

The Complete Memoirs of George Sherston
by Siegfried Sassoon
An autobiographical account of Sassoon's life before and during the First World War. Sassoon has changed the names of the characters and George Sherston (Sassoon) is not a poet. This trilogy (made up of *Memoirs of a Fox Hunting Man, Memoirs of an Infantry Officer* and *Sherston's Progress*) demonstrates the effects of the war on both the serving soldiers and those left at home.

For a list of the fictional characters and their factual counterparts, see Appendix II of *Siegfried Sassoon by John Stuart Roberts*.

These books and others may be purchased through our Web site bookstore at: www.greatwarliterature.co.uk/bookstore.html

BIBLIOGRAPHY

The Collected Poems of Edward Thomas
Edited by R George Thomas

Anthem for Doomed Youth
by Jon Stallworthy

Violets from Oversea
by Tonie and Valmai Hart

Minds at War - The Poetry and Experience of the First World War
Edited by David Roberts

The War Poets
by Robert Giddings

Poems of the First World War - Never Such Innocence
Edited by Martin Stephen

Lads
by Martin Taylor

Siegfried Sassoon: The Making of a War Poet
A Biography 1886-1918
by Jean Moorcroft Wilson

Siegfried Sassoon
by John Stuart Roberts

Siegfried Sassoon - Collected Poems 1908-1956

Siegfried Sassoon - The War Poems
Arranged and Introduced by Rupert Hart-Davis

Up the Line to Death: The War Poets 1914-1918
Edited by Brian Gardner

Stars in a Dark Night: The Letters of Ivor Gurney to the Chapman Family
by Anthony Boden

Wilfred Owen - War Poems and Others
Edited with an Introduction and Notes by Dominic Hibberd

www.britishlegion.org.uk

www.greatwar.co.uk

www.vac-acc.gc.ca/general
Office Web site for Canadian Veterans Affairs

OTHER GREAT WAR LITERATURE STUDY GUIDE TITLES

Paperback Books

Birdsong	ISBN 1905378238
Journey's End	ISBN 1905378165
Regeneration	ISBN 190537822X
Strange Meeting	ISBN 1905378211
Female Poets of the First World War - Volume One	ISBN 1905378254
The Return of the Soldier	ISBN 1905378351

Great War Literature Study Guide E-Books (Electronic Books)on:

Novels & Plays

Birdsong	ISBN 1905378181
Journey's End	ISBN 1905378173
Regeneration	ISBN 190537819X
Strange Meeting	ISBN 1905378203
The Return of the Soldier	ISBN 190537836X

Poets

Harold Begbie	ISBN 1905378262
Rupert Brooke	ISBN 1905378033
Female War Poets 1	ISBN 1905378114
Female War Poets 2	ISBN 1905378327
Female War Poets 3	ISBN 1905378270
Wilfrid Wilson Gibson	ISBN 1905378149
Julian Grenfell	ISBN 1905378084
E A Mackintosh	ISBN 1905378335
John McCrae	ISBN 1905378157
Robert Nichols	ISBN 1905378025
Wilfred Owen	ISBN 1905378017
Jessie Pope	ISBN 1905378106
Isaac Rosenberg	ISBN 1905378130

Siegfried Sassoon	ISBN 1905378041
Charles Hamilton Sorley	ISBN 1905378092
Edward Thomas	ISBN 1905378122
Robert Ernest Vernède	ISBN 1905378297
Arthur Graeme West	ISBN 1905378289